M000028220

One-Minute
PRAYERS®
for a
WOMAN'S YEAR

Hope Lyda

HARVEST HOUSE PUBLISHERS
EUGENE, OREGON

Unless otherwise indicated, all Scripture quotations are from the Holy Bible, New International Version®, NIV®. Copyright © 1973, 1978, 1984, 2011 by Biblica, Inc.® Used by permission. All rights reserved worldwide.

Verses marked ICB are from the International Children's Bible®. Copyright © 1986, 1988, 1999 by Thomas Nelson, Inc. Used by permission. All rights reserved.

Cover design by Bryce Williamson

Cover photo © Maria_Galybina / Gettyimages

Interior design by KUHN Design Group

Some material previously published in *One-Minute Prayers® to End Your Day*, *One-Minute Prayers® for Women*, *One-Minute Prayers® for Singles*, and *One-Minute Prayers® from the Bible*.

ONE-MINUTE PRAYERS is a registered trademark of The Hawkins Children's LLC. Harvest House Publishers, Inc., is the exclusive licensee of the federally registered trademark ONE-MINUTE PRAYERS.

One-Minute Prayers® for a Woman's Year

Published by Harvest House Publishers
Eugene, Oregon 97408
www.harvesthousepublishers.com

ISBN 978-0-7369-7460-8 (hardcover)
ISBN 978-0-7369-7461-5 (eBook)

Printed in China

20 21 22 23 24 25 26 27 / RDS-SK / 10 9 8 7 6 5 4 3 2 1

Contents

Anticipation and Hope 4

Truth and Love 35

Abundance and Provision 65

Trust and Faith 94

Comfort and Presence 124

Purpose and Fulfillment 154

Relationships and Connection 184

Healing and Shelter 215

Help and Encouragement 246

Confidence and Inspiration 276

Praise and Dependence 308

Plans and Prayers 338

About the Author

Hope Lyda has written devotionals, novels, and prayer books that have sold more than a million copies. She has worked in publishing for more than 20 years, writing and coming alongside other writers to help them shape their heart messages. As a trained spiritual director, she loves to help others enter God's presence and pay attention to what is unfolding in their lives.

SELECT TITLES BY HOPE LYDA

My Unedited Writing Year
One-Minute Prayers® to Unwind a Worried Mind
One-Minute Prayers® to Start Your Day
One-Minute Prayers® for Hope and Comfort
One-Minute Prayers® for Young Women
One-Minute Prayers® for Women

|

Designer Hope

*For in him all things were created: things in heaven
and on earth, visible and invisible, whether
thrones or powers or rulers or authorities; all things
have been created through him and for him.*

COLOSSIANS 1:16

have come to realize that as universal as your love is,
Lord, you are very specific in how you speak to me
and how you lead me.

You have given me a faith that is mine. You invite
me to a hope and faith designed by you that serves my
journey. From the very beginning, you crafted my life.
Your name is emblazoned on my heart. Your hands
have tailored my body and spirit and continue to shape
who I am becoming. Lord, I am grateful to witness
what it looks like, feels like to walk the path created for
me. I carry with me the hope and faith you have given
to me, and I embark on the journey uniquely created
to serve you.

2

The Journey to Hope

*When you have entered the land the LORD your God is
giving you as an inheritance and have taken possession
of it and settled in it, take some of the firstfruits of all
that you produce from the soil of the land the LORD your
God is giving you and put them in a basket. Then go to
the place the LORD your God will choose as a dwelling
for his Name and say to the priest in office at the time,
"I declare today to the LORD your God that I have come
to the land the LORD swore to our forefathers to give us."*

DEUTERONOMY 26:1-3

You are the God of promises. I receive an inheritance of hope and possibility because you give to your children an expanse of life to cultivate. I may not own a plot of land, but I do have permission to care for this life, tend to it, and seek your will for its harvest.

I exist because of the generations of my family before me. My faith and hope exist because of my salvation in you. Today I will take some of the firstfruits from these legacies and enter my future with proof of your goodness.

3

Calling Out to You

From the ends of the earth I call to you,
I call as my heart grows faint;
lead me to the rock that is higher than I.
For you have been my refuge,
a strong tower against the foe.

PSALM 61:2-3

Even in the most confusing times of my life, I have been able to call out to you with a heart filled with hope. When I can barely keep my eyes open another minute because I am weary, you lead me to a place where I can rest. When I am afraid, you calm my spirit and show me the view ahead that is clear and secure.

For as long as I have known you, I have had a sense of your love. I know it is okay to be here, in this moment, and not know what will happen tomorrow. Each day you lead me to a place higher than the day before.

4

Always My Hope

You have been my hope, Sovereign LORD,
my confidence since my youth.

PSALM 71:5

When I first came to know you personally, Lord, I stood so tall. I had unshakable faith in your mightiness. When I am around a new believer, I feel that excitement once again. Restore this confidence, Lord. I will turn to the wisdom of your Word and infuse my life with the security of your promises.

Thank you, Lord, for the power you extend to me. The small windows of opportunity I once perceived are now wide-open doors. Everything is better when I stand in your confidence. Fortify my life with the strength of your plan. As I rise up to claim my hope in you, let me stand tall…just as I did in the youth of my faith.

5

Faithfulness

A longing fulfilled is sweet to the soul.
PROVERBS 13:19

God, you are so faithful to me. Your goodness surrounds me daily. I asked for help today, and you answered me in surprising ways. I felt vulnerable and needed a sense of protection and care—and you were there. I have longed for this kind of security all my life. Even with faith, I often doubted that you might be there to catch me should I fall.

But today I realized the hunger is gone and fulfillment is in its place. You have met my longing with the sweetness of a future and a hope.

6

Rushing to Do Good

*Who is going to harm you
if you are eager to do good?*

1 PETER 3:13

can get ahead of myself when trying to do good. I
anticipate the rewards of the situation. I see how one
giving moment can turn a bad situation into a blessing. There is the power to change lives and hearts when
I act on the impulse to serve you. Lord, direct these
urges to do good so that I serve your higher purpose
and not my own.

You smile upon a child who desires to please you,
who is eager to please her Father. Your love embraces
me and holds me close to the security of your mercy.
How can I not be excited to share this comfort and
holiness with other people? I hope you are proud of
your girl.

7

Counting on You

For what you have done I will always praise you…
I will hope in your name,
for your name is good.

PSALM 52:9

When I speak of your name and praise you for what you have given to me and brought me through, some people don't know how to respond. It makes them uncomfortable because they have not experienced the same. They have been let down by people; therefore, it's hard for them to imagine a God who does not fail, who does not leave.

I want to share hope in you. Grant me a gentle spirit and give me an understanding heart so that I might show your goodness through my actions and my continued praise.

8

Pray It, Don't Say It

*Keep this Book of the Law always on your lips;
meditate on it day and night, so that you may
be careful to do everything written in it. Then
you will be prosperous and successful.*

JOSHUA 1:8

My mouth has been eager to talk of your mercy and your truth, but I am not good at meditating on your wisdom and your law. I select bits of your Word as I need it to prove a point or to demonstrate my knowledge. How silly I can be. This is not serving you, and it is not leading me to the purpose and prosperity you long to give me.

Only when I own your truths deep within my mind, heart, and spirit can they produce fruit in my life. Only when I commit to holding your character in esteem will I have the hope of becoming more like you.

9

A New Dance

I will build you up again, Virgin Israel, and
you will be rebuilt. Again you will take up your
timbrels and go out to dance with the joyful.

JEREMIAH 31:4

You are rebuilding me right now, Lord. I feel the growing pains. I see the unnecessary pieces of my life fall away. I watch as my new life emerges from the dust of construction. It is hard to be carved into a new being, Lord. Be gentle with me as you mold me into a creation that serves you even better. I have hope in what you have for me.

There will be a day in the near future when I will dance. Music will flow through my life and give me a reason to shout with great happiness. God, please keep working on me. Your vision for my life is worth the wait.

10

With Your Hand

*You open your hand
and satisfy the desires of every living thing.*

PSALM 145:16

With your hand you shape the sky and earth. You plan the days of many and orchestrate how the lives intersect and create community. Everything big and small is managed by you. I don't always come to you with my desires. I feel selfish or self-centered to say that I want the love of others.

Yet when my heart has been broken, it is your hand that molds the pieces back into the shape of hope. I believe in the goodness that comes from your hands.

11

Said It Before

Yes, my soul, find rest in God;
my hope comes from him.

PSALM 62:5

I f I have told myself once, I have told myself a million times: It is you alone who gives me hope. People can let me down. My lofty goals fail me. Even my hard work doesn't always produce the results I envision. Lord, my soul and my spirit were born of your grace, and they will only find hope within your embrace.

I wonder what my later years will be like. Will I find happiness? Sorrow? Peace? All of these? Today, with faith, I understand that it won't matter what the future brings. My soul will find rest and hope in your limitless love.

12

24/7 Hope

Guide me in your truth and teach me,
for you are God my Savior,
and my hope is in you all day long.

PSALM 25:5

My love for you is as deep as the day is long. My hand reaches as far as it can to touch your face. My feet step forth with the desire to follow your paths. Lord, you guide me and gently navigate my steps. When I am lost, you bring me back into the safety of your pasture.

My hope is in you all day long because you care for me. When I wasn't a person of faith, you lovingly protected me and brought me into this place of strength and possibility. Lord, I pray for my hope to multiply so that I might bring a Christlike attitude into my life in every way.

13

I'm Waiting

I wait for the LORD, my whole being waits,
and in his word I put my hope.

PSALM 130:5

It isn't easy. I had a plan for how my life would look and feel by this age. Those things have not happened, and I find myself waiting patiently. Okay, not so patiently. The clock of "want" ticks with every passing day. Every part of me longs for the achievement and success I had planned.

God, take from me the desires that are not of you. Place my hope in the eternal wonder of your perfect plan. Waiting is only wasting time if it does not lead me to you.

14

Hearing the Voice

*A voice of one calling in the desert, "Prepare the
way for the Lord, make straight paths for him."*

MATTHEW 3:3

When I was young, I didn't always heed the advice
of my parents. And as I grew, there were times
when I ignored guidance from those who knew the
way. I have shrugged off wisdom and walked in another
direction.

But when I heard the instruction to prepare my
heart for you, I was ready to listen. My childhood resistances, my mild or significant rebellions, my human
desire for self-reliance were no match for the hope of
a faith and a future. Help me continue to prepare my
heart and life for the lessons you have to teach me, Lord.
I am eager to hear you.

15

Insight

*This is my prayer: that your love may abound more
and more in knowledge and depth of insight, so
that you may be able to discern what is best and
may be pure and blameless for the day of Christ.*

PHILIPPIANS 1:9-10

have a friend who has great instinct for what to do or
what to say at any given moment. Meanwhile, I take
a step back, afraid that I might do the wrong thing and
make the situation worse. I want my first response to
all people and situations, difficulties and dream possibilities, to be made with the hope and confidence I
have in you.

Infuse me with courage and insight, Lord. I know
it is my own insecurity that keeps me back in the shadows and holds me in a pattern of indecision. This also
prevents me from demonstrating your love and your
power to others in my life. Tomorrow, I will step out
in faith in some way. It is time to live in your knowledge with confidence.

16

What Comes Next

*Therefore, with minds that are alert and fully
sober, set your hope on the grace to be brought to
you when Jesus Christ is revealed at his coming.*

1 PETER 1:13

I get so caught up in asking questions about what will
happen next that I forget to ask for your help in the
moment. All day today my mind was overflowing with
scenarios of the future. I tried to make decisions based
on hypothetical situations. It was exhausting.

Now I am asking for your strength, self-control,
and hope to face my present. Only when I seek your
grace and vision for my life will I ever be prepared for
whatever tomorrow brings. Remind me to pause, Lord,
and to prepare my mind and my heart by being sure of
and confident in your mercy. Your love is the answer
to all of my questions.

17

Love Is

May your unfailing love be with us, LORD,
even as we put our hope in you.

PSALM 33:22

Love is unfailing and uncompromising. Your love is a shining star in the night's sky that leads us forward and toward the hope of tomorrow. You know my steps before I ponder which way to go. You offer me free will so that I can choose to follow my Creator in love and submission.

For too long, I looked to money and possessions and four walls to prepare me for my tomorrows. Yet none of these grant me lasting security; that only comes from you, Lord. Help me to never invest myself and my faith in the things of the world. I will place my hope in you.

18

Nourishment from Your Table

*You prepare a table before me
in the presence of my enemies.*

PSALM 23:5

When I face the opposition of the enemy, Lord, I can run to the table you are preparing for me. I am seated beside you—and I drink of your wisdom, I dine on your truth, and I am satisfied. I am saved here at your table. My enemies and worries fade in the presence of my Host.

At each sitting I am nourished by your banquet. When I leave the table to face my day, your goodness follows me. I am filled with your satisfying love. When I fear my enemies, I think of the security of your eternal home. I shake my head in amazement that you promise to protect me, prepare the way for me, and reserve a place for me at the table of your grace. You welcome me into your presence, and I am blessed.

19

Inner Strength

I rise before dawn and cry for help;
I have put my hope in your word.

PSALM 119:147

Lord, you make me a survivor. It is by your grace that I have walked through hard times in order to experience joy, peace, or change on the other side. I hold tightly to the peace I have in you. Even in the early days of my youth, when I didn't know what to call you, I knew of your hope. It was built into my spirit, woven into my DNA.

Thank you, Lord. When I rise in the morning, you are present. I meet you in your Word and discover sustenance for my day and my life. You. I am forever grateful that I can tap into the inner hope of your Spirit. Praise you, Lord.

20

A Room of My Own

*In my Father's house are many rooms; if that were
not so, would I have told you that I am going there
to prepare a place for you? And if I go and prepare
a place for you, I will come back and take you to
be with me that you also may be where I am.*

JOHN 14:2-3

I remember the first time I had my own room. I felt
a sense of being cared for and provided for. Lord, I
spent so much time preparing every detail in order to
make it unquestionably mine. I think of this experience when I read your promise to prepare a room for
me. A place for me in heaven's glory.

When you take me home and show me this room,
I am certain it will reflect how well you know my
heart. The walls will be the shade of happiness. The
fabrics will be woven with threads of loving memories.
It will shimmer with your splendor. I will run into it
gladly, eager to be in your presence forever. And I will
know that the Master of the house prepared this room
because I am unquestionably his.

21

But by Faith

"If you can'?" said Jesus. "Everything is possible for the one who believes."

MARK 9:23

Patience is not one of my strengths, Lord. It is a virtue I hope to develop as my faith grows and as I understand my life in your will. It is my faith that enables me to wait at all. I impatiently wait for growth, an answer, a sign, a finger coming out of the heavens to point the way. Such a list!

Help me to rest in your Spirit and in the faith I have placed in you, my Lord. I pray for true righteousness—the kind that comes from perseverance. When I am tested by trials and even doubt, may I be a woman of conviction and commitment. You not only see me through, but also carry me through these times. You turn my times of waiting into moments of moving forward.

22

Opening a Gift

*Since you are eager for gifts of the Spirit, try
to excel in those that build up the church.*

1 CORINTHIANS 14:12

God, grant me spiritual gifts that serve your body.
In the past I have prayed for gifts that would help
me succeed in different areas of my life. I wanted to
give you glory, but I didn't understand how the gifts I
receive are meant to be given back to you and the family of believers.

The gifts you plant in my soul will emerge as I am
ready to use them for good. May I never misinterpret
your blessings as permission to serve myself. While I
anticipate the strengths you plan for my life, give me
vision to recognize the spiritual gifts of other people
so that I may share your hope with them and see you
more clearly in those around me.

23

Hope for Me

*By faith we eagerly await through the Spirit
the righteousness for which we hope.*

GALATIANS 5:5

When flashbacks from days of old produce images of me making mistakes, missing opportunities, and stumbling over obstacles I created, it is easy to take on shame. Through the lens of today, it is tough for me to understand why I did some of the things I did or reacted to situations and relationships with such frustration. I realize that back then I was constantly afraid to lose face, be wrong, be rejected, be alone.

Lord, you remind me how much I have grown since then. Now, instead of trying to hide my transgressions, I bring them to you with faith in transformation. My faith is moving me toward righteousness, but it will be your grace that gets me there. I'm starting to believe there is hope for me yet.

24

Waiting for Your Presence

LORD, I wait for you;
you will answer, Lord my God.

PSALM 38:15

My heart beats rapidly waiting for your presence, Lord. I have called out to you in a moment of great need. I am so empty right now. I do not long for the conversation or advice of friends. I only want to be resting in your hand. You know me so well. You see the places of my heart and my life that I hold back from the world, and you love me.

My lips form the name of my Savior because you are the sole Source of unconditional love. When I am emptied of energy and desire, I ask to be swept away to your refuge. Just when I cannot be alone with my anxiety and humanity any longer, you answer my cries. Your mercy rushes over my worry and fills me with peace.

25

Running on Low

You wearied yourself by such going about,
but you would not say, "It is hopeless."
You found renewal of your strength,
and so you did not faint.

ISAIAH 57:10

always dreamed of being a respected, productive woman with many responsibilities. But my imaginings shone the spotlight on a false picture of the calm, collected, posed and poised, well-dressed version of myself. But in reality, Lord, the tasks and commitments involved in being a successful woman can become tedious. I grow weary.

When I am running on low, I run to the Most High. Lord, refresh my spirit today. Infuse my body and soul with your limitless strength and might. When my legs are about to buckle from the weight of real and perceived obligations, remind me to embrace the plan you have for my life. I need to give you what is on my plate every day. Only then will my steps be strong enough to carry me on the right path.

26

A Place of Peace

"The glory of this present house will be greater than the glory of the former house," declares the LORD Almighty. "And in this place I will grant peace," declares the LORD Almighty.

HAGGAI 2:9

This time in my life is not like any other time before. This place along my journey will be greater than any other because I know you better. I have held on to you through the difficulties and the delights. You have carried me from past times of trial into present times of peace.

While I have sought peace from other sources, I knew they were temporary solutions for eternal needs. That is never a match. But when I discovered you, I began a journey to a new place—a place of hope and promise that rests in your embrace.

27

Foot in Mouth

Who among the gods is like you, LORD? Who is like you—
majestic in holiness, awesome in glory, working wonders?

EXODUS 15:11

Show them, God!" Sometimes I scream this in my mind when standing around people with hardened hearts who do not understand the essence of life and who work against goodness. I call out to you like you are Superman. Save them. Save us. Save me.

You are all-powerful, Lord, so show them. Show these people who do not know pure love and forgiveness what your grace is all about. Change the hearts of those who have bad intentions and who are self-destructive. Reveal your awesome wonders to everyone so that they never question your existence. I want my peers, my friends, and the people I walk by on the street to sense your majesty and glory.

This is when you return my command back to me, and I am humbled. Hear my new prayer today, Lord: "Help me show them you."

28

This Very Purpose

*I have raised you up for this very purpose, that
I might show you my power and that my name
might be proclaimed in all the earth.*

EXODUS 9:16

Will I ever feel as though I have arrived? When I was a child I could not wait until adulthood. I thought all the mysteries of life would become known. And I was certain a sense of deliberate purpose would fill me. I am still not at this place of understanding, Lord. But I do know your love.

Lord, work out your will in me and through me. Make my days fruitful. Guide me in my choices and in my attitude as I become the person you created me to be. Let me carry on with purpose, trusting in your love.

29

Stay or Go?

In him we were also chosen, having been predestined according to the plan of him who works out everything in conformity with the purpose of his will, in order that we, who were the first to hope in Christ, might be for the praise of his glory.

EPHESIANS 1:11-12

As I question my current direction in life, Lord, I ask you to shine your light on the way I am to go. If I am on track, I need to stop doubting my circumstances just because I am not fulfilled. I will not have an excuse to wallow in self-pity any longer. I promise to keep on the path you give me.

I know you care about every step I take. My direction does matter. And my fulfillment directly relates to your higher purpose for my life. Let me rest in your love and your proven faithfulness. If this direction is the right one, then I sing your praises, Lord. Let me know, Lord: Do I stay or go?

30

Become Wise

Take notice, you senseless ones among the people;
you fools, when will you become wise?

PSALM 94:8

Just when I am feeling confident in myself and my abilities, I realize that I get through my busy days relying mainly on wit and quick thinking. At best, my skill involves strategic decision-making. But, Lord, I need your wisdom. Life presents so many baffling changes and circumstances that my foolish, just-getting-by ways present me with little comfort and guidance.

Lead me in the ways of wisdom. I want to be your pupil, Lord. I will turn to your Word and will seek your face as I strive to leave foolishness behind.

31

As the Storm Passes

*[Jesus] got up and rebuked the wind and the
raging waters; the storm subsided, and all was
calm. "Where is your faith?" he asked his disciples.*

LUKE 8:24-25

When the air stirs about me, when the wind blows from all directions, when I cannot stand because of the pressure around me…I want to be a person of faith. My eyes peer toward the dark night, and I cannot distinguish shapes. There is so much left unknown. Yet my heart does not race and my mind does not doubt because I know where my faith is—it is in the hope of the moment, it is in the belief that the storm will pass, it is in the assurance that your peace overcomes everything I will face.

32

Show Me

I have chosen the way of truth;
I have set my heart on your laws.

PSALM 119:30

I am so thankful I discovered truth when I did. I was all over the place seeking answers to random questions. I didn't even know what to ask in my quest for understanding and identity. You raised me out of my ignorance and showed me the light of your heart. Everything clicked at that moment.

I still have times of confusion. I still have obstacles to overcome, but never without a measure of truth to guide me. Now my many questions are replaced by one request: Show me the way, Lord.

33

Absolutes

*We know also that the Son of God has come and has
given us understanding, so that we may know him who
is true. And we are in him who is true by being in his
Son Jesus Christ. He is the true God and eternal life.*

1 JOHN 5:20

Lord, do you see all the ways women are invited to
falseness? A pretentious attitude and a modified
appearance will get you far. That is what the world
offers. No wonder so many women and young girls
struggle with a sense of self. Your love grounds your
children in truth about their worth. We are all valu-
able because we are yours.

Even if I cannot always tell which world image is
real or retouched, I know the image of the cross is true.
I can believe in you completely.

34

Words of Truth

Jesus answered, "I am the way and the truth and the life. No one comes to the Father except through me. If you really know me, you will know my Father as well. From now on, you do know him and have seen him."

JOHN 14:6-7

To be able to see you, Lord, is a blessing. Reading your Word provides me with a picture of your character, your nature, your love. While faith can be defined as belief in something unseen, my faith in you goes beyond that. I do see you. In the beauty of the earth, in the smile of a child, and in each victory of justice, I see your face.

Each day I try to know Christ better. It is my way to move closer to the truth of creation and the truth of eternity. I am stronger than ever before because I follow this quest for a deeper understanding of you and your Son.

35

Self-Deception

*If we claim to be without sin, we deceive
ourselves and the truth is not in us.*

1 John 1:8

To maintain my sense of status in the world, I sometimes build myself up with half-truths. I have moments when I would rather believe lies than seek your truth. I am weak in that way. But the bottom always falls out from beneath plans based in deception. Sooner or later I end up back at the foot of the cross.

I have such sin, Lord. When I compare my human fickleness to your godly steadfastness, I am ashamed. But there is redemption in faith that is grounded in your goodness. I return to you and your unchanging truth.

36

All of the Above

*Do you know how God controls the clouds
and makes his lightning flash?
Do you know how the clouds hang poised,
those wonders of him who has perfect knowledge?*

JOB 37:15-16

When other people ask about you, I am at a loss for words and answers. Like taking quizzes in high school when I was always tempted to answer "all of the above" or "none of the above," I look for a blanket statement that saves my face and faith. I pray to be a more faithful reader and prayer of your Word so that I do not miss the opportunities before me to deepen my faith and that of other people.

For now my "all of the above" answer to faith-and-life questions is "it's all from above." The answers are all with you and from you and of you. That knowledge is really all any of us need to hold on to.

37

Direct My Steps

*Then Saul prayed to the Lord, the God of
Israel, "Give me the right answer."*

1 SAMUEL 14:41 ICB

Lord, is this one of those times when any choice is okay with you, as long as I stay in your ways and wisdom? Or is this really a fork in the road that has a blatant "of God" and "not of God" option? Forgive me for not having this understanding. I am still learning to communicate with you and learning to hear the discerning voice of your Spirit.

Please direct my feet, my mouth, my heart so that I follow in the way that is right for me and for your will. I pray as Saul did. Give me the right answer, Lord.

38

Your Ingredients

Your hands made me and formed me;
give me understanding to learn your commands.

PSALM 119:73

I thank you today and every day for shaping me, forming my very spirit and soul, Lord. I have come to know you so personally because my heart has desired to return to its Maker. This longing leads me back to you over and over, even when I wander and follow a path of my own creation.

I am made with your ingredients. My strengths and weaknesses all blend together beneath your hand so that I become this complex self. I know whose hand created me. Now I pray for the knowledge to understand and follow your commands. This complex being you made as "me" has been created just for this life, for these very personal circumstances and choices. May I follow your commands so that your creation is used for the purposes you intended.

39

Willing Student

Teach me knowledge and good judgment,
for I trust your commands.
Before I was afflicted I went astray,
but now I obey your word.

PSALM 119:66-67

I want to be taught by the Master. Remind me each day how precious time is and how much I still have to learn about faith and life from my Creator. My willingness to invest in my spiritual education must begin now. I believe in your Word and your wisdom. Please help me pay attention to your commands. When I want to glide through days on end without learning, bring my heart to attention.

Lord, I will need help following through with this discipline, but I am eager to study and obey your Word. Share your knowledge with this willing student.

40

All Is Fair

Then you will understand what is right and just
and fair—every good path.
For wisdom will enter your heart,
and knowledge will be pleasant to your soul.
Discretion will protect you,
and understanding will guard you.

PROVERBS 2:9-11

Live and let live. To each his own. All is fair in love and war. Lord, these actually were philosophies I was clinging to as I made my way from yesterday to today. I created all kinds of theories that gave me breathing room and allowed me to not take responsibility for the fairness or unfairness of the situations in which I played a role.

Fill me with the wisdom that sees past my own nose and interests. Move me through circumstances so that I can feel the joy of knowledge that embraces justice and compassion. May I guard my heart with discretion and discernment so the philosophies of old do not shape my understanding and my perspective again.

41

Go Right Ahead

I will keep my eyes always on the LORD.
With him at my right hand, I will not be shaken.

PSALM 16:8

Lord, go before me and create a path for me to follow. I give my days ahead to you and your service. Instruct me as I eat, sleep, and pray so that I am not filled with questions that can lead me astray in a weak moment. You are the Model of the heart I long for. You are my Counselor and Redeemer who knows the way through the mountains and canyons.

I take each step with my eyes on your might. Let my commitment of faith be transformed into wisdom and love. And may I never be so sure of my pace that I desire to pass you and take over the lead on this journey.

42

Shed the Light

Who can discern their own errors?
Forgive my hidden faults.

PSALM 19:12

Nobody really wants to know their faults, especially if it means that other people can see them too. But I am beginning to understand why it is so important to understand my problems, my flaws, my weaknesses. God, you are my safe place. I pray for you to gently reveal those areas in which I can be stronger, kinder, more aware.

I desire to live a life that is pleasing to you. I know this does not happen overnight. Give me the blessings of insight and discernment. Only when I accept these blessings can I truly embrace who I am in you.

43

Before the Rain

Do the skies themselves send down showers?
No, it is you, LORD our God.
Therefore our hope is in you,
for you are the one who does all this.

JEREMIAH 14:22

When the surge of a spring rain passes by, I am eager to breath in the fresh air. The sprinkles might be inconvenient. My plans might change. But I am thankful that the clouds bring renewal to a thirsty earth. I realize that before I hear the first drops on my roof, you first commanded the showers. You are behind everything beautiful and wondrous.

I and all the universe benefit from your sweet rain and the replenishment it brings. When the clouds come, I learn a lesson about hope: It is to be placed in you, the maker of the smallest and the largest blessings.

44

In Your Hands

I form the light and create darkness,
I bring prosperity and create disaster;
I, the LORD, do all these things.

ISAIAH 45:7

t is so easy to take credit for accomplishments or milestones in my life. Yet it is you who formed the light and created darkness. This morning I found myself accepting praise for something that was entirely your doing.

My heart lesson today is to give you glory for all that happens. You, Lord, do all that is good in my life and throughout my days. I cheat myself out of a deeper faith when I take credit for wonders shaped by my Creator.

45

Seed of Faith

I would like to learn just one thing from
you: Did you receive the Spirit by the
law, or by believing what you heard?

GALATIANS 3:2

Does my faith reveal a strong sense of your saving grace and your love? I ask because lately my motives seem so much about bringing justice to situations and relationships. I first came to you because of your compassion and your forgiveness, so why do I seem determined to pass judgment rather than to give mercy?

Help me learn to treat others with the love you have shown me. Maybe I will plant the seed of faith in another's heart.

46

Always My Teacher

When [Jesus] had finished washing their feet, he put on his clothes and returned to his place. "Do you understand what I have done for you?" he asked them. "You call me 'Teacher' and 'Lord,' and rightly so, for that is what I am. Now that I, your Lord and Teacher, have washed your feet, you also should wash one another's feet. I have set you an example that you should do as I have done for you."

JOHN 13:12-15

The role models of faith around me are people who keep learning from you. Give me a hunger for the lessons you have to teach me. I want to follow your example with passion and purpose. When you washed the feet of your disciples, you did not call them to praise you, but to turn around and wash the feet of others. This is your powerful lesson to your children. May I become a forever student of the Master.

47

Ritual

*Every morning and evening they present burnt
offerings and fragrant incense to the LORD.*

2 CHRONICLES 13:11

gave you my day today, Lord. With great intention, I handed over my emotions, my worries, my work, my relationships, and my steps. I feel the difference as the day comes to a close. I am more aware of how you are a part of all that I am, do, say, and feel. Oh, how many days I have wasted by not being aware of this truth!

Help me give my day to you again tomorrow. May I start and end all my days by presenting to you the offering of my life, of myself. And may this sacrifice be pleasing to you.

Forecast

*[Jesus] replied, "When evening comes, you say, 'It will
be fair weather, for the sky is red,' and in the morning,
'Today it will be stormy, for the sky is red and overcast.'
You know how to interpret the appearance of the
sky, but you cannot interpret the signs of the times."*

MATTHEW 16:2-3

love to check the weather forecasts for the week.
When I gather all the facts, God, I feel more in control. I receive a sense of security. Getting the temper-
atures, examining the details, and knowing how the
clouds will cover the sky might help me plan a family
picnic, but that does not give me your full knowledge
or your power.

I don't have to know what the weather is for tomorrow. Life is not built on predictions. It is built on your
truth, rain or shine.

49

Loose Change

*Do not forget to do good and to share with
others, for with such sacrifices God is pleased.*

HEBREWS 13:16

When I come home, I reach into my pockets or
pour from my wallet any coins remaining from
a day of spending. These leftover portions I once considered hardly worth saving can actually add up to a
significant amount. That is the power of accumulation.
This view gives me a stronger sense of appreciation for
the small portions. The smallest offerings matter.

Lord, help me be aware of how my smallest offerings of kindness and generosity matter. Show me ways
to spend goodness and forgiveness on others throughout the day. May I never consider a portion of kindness too small or insignificant to receive or give. I know
that each act of compassion accumulates in the hearts
of others and in your purpose.

50

Counting Before Sleep

How precious to me are your thoughts, God!
How vast is the sum of them!
Were I to count them,
they would outnumber the grains of sand—
When I awake, I am still with you.

PSALM 139:17-18

After a day of multitasking and problem solving, I have a hard time unwinding. My thoughts can rev up, spiral down, or pull me toward energy when I would rather be resting. I turn to you and seek your thoughts, God. Fill my mind and my heart with your peaceful, living words. When I call out to you, you are there.

Starting my day, living my day, and closing my day with you, Lord, gives me the peace I've longed to know. When my eyes are wide open to take in all the blessings, you are there. When my eyes are closed and rest is nourishing my body and spirit, you are there too. How precious you are to me.

51

The Seeing Blind

Like the blind we grope along the wall,
feeling our way like people without eyes.

ISAIAH 59:10

When I am not tapped into the Spirit, I let demands, schedules, and requests direct my steps. I grasp for anything that appears to be stable but am often deceived. Help me reach out for you as I stumble along.

Let me draw on the wisdom of your Spirit. I want to rely on your truth to lead me forward. I do not want to walk like a blind man, when I have been given your gift of sight through your leading. May I be strong enough to resist the pull of the world's demands and walk straight and steady.

52

A Vessel for Truth

*What we have received is not the spirit of the world,
but the Spirit who is from God, so that we may
understand what God has freely given us. This is
what we speak, not in words taught us by human
wisdom but in words taught by the Spirit, expressing
spiritual realities with Spirit-taught words.*

1 CORINTHIANS 2:12-13

Lord, give me the words to say to other people. Let me speak from the Spirit to encourage them, lead them, and direct them to faith. You give me the Spirit freely. May I draw upon this source of strength and peace in all circumstances. My joys will brighten; my sorrows will lighten. I praise you, my Creator and Redeemer, for you are worthy of praise. I long to become a vessel for your spiritual truths. May these truths flow through me in words of wisdom. I rest in the peace growing stronger within me every day.

53

Tap Into the Gift

Let the message of Christ dwell among you richly as
you teach and admonish one another with all wisdom
through psalms, hymns, and spiritual songs from the
Spirit, singing to God with gratitude in your hearts.

COLOSSIANS 3:16

You are my hiding place, Lord. You also dwell within my spirit. When I live on the surface and ride the wave of materialism, I miss out on using the gift of your inner teachings. I want my wisdom to be based on your truth. I want to share with other people without a sense of personal importance. Use me, my Lord. Strip me of my self-dependence, and cause me to rely solely on you.

I have such gratitude in my heart because of your goodness. I want my soul to be a place that welcomes grace and returns it to the world through kindness and compassion. Let my song of living ring with truth and resound within the hearts of other people.

54

Bad Influences

Do not be misled: "Bad company corrupts good character." Come back to your senses as you ought, and stop sinning; for there are some who are ignorant of God—I say this to your shame.

1 CORINTHIANS 15:33-34

should have trusted the still, small voice within today. I felt it even before I heard it. Then I coughed to drown out the sound, made a commotion to distract my spirit, and headed into the fray of a bad day—a bad day that just got worse. I participated in gossip; I let negativity override a sense of accomplishment; I pretended I was responsible for my own worth.

Lord, protect my heart from negative influences. May I resist giving myself over to false praise, pride, and words that tear down other people. My heart is better than that because it is yours. I will honor you with intentional effort tomorrow, Lord. I promise to let that inner voice speak to my life.

55

Always

Love is patient, love is kind. It does not envy, it does not boast, it is not proud. It does not dishonor others, it is not self-seeking, it is not easily angered, it keeps no record of wrongs. Love does not delight in evil but rejoices with the truth. It always protects, always trusts, always hopes, always perseveres.

1 CORINTHIANS 13:4-7

I hear the "Love is" verses every time I go to a wedding. It moves me each time. My heart can get caught up in which attributes are missing in my life right now, but underneath that ache is peace. I have experienced the purest love straight from you, the Creator of love himself. You have shown me selfless, truthful, and sweet love.

In my life, I have directly seen your hand of protection and guidance. Never in my moments of loss or pain have I felt alone. And best of all, I do believe that love is that gift in my heart that allows me to always hope.

56

The Strength of Love

Be on your guard; stand firm in the faith; be courageous; be strong. Do everything in love.

1 CORINTHIANS 16:13-14

I t isn't easy to love. There are some people who seem difficult to embrace with warmth and kindness. I lose sight of how to love when I am around them. I have even caught myself being a bit indifferent toward those I know you call me to love.

Expand my view of what love is. Stretch the limited walls of my human heart to make room for everybody I am meant to care for. Direct my actions so I act courageously on behalf of those in need. Allow me to stand firmly on the foundation of love.

57

Love for All

*The LORD is righteous in all his ways
and faithful in all he does.
The LORD is near to all who call on him,
to all who call on him in truth.*

PSALM 145:17-18

Why am I so careful about whom I love? When I face the chance to make a new friend, I am thankful…but I am also hesitant. I'm afraid of what that commitment might mean. If I meet a stranger in need, I hold back my smile and my willingness to extend grace. Fear keeps me from loving as you love. My busyness holds me back from opening my heart and home to others.

You are near to me and to those who call out your name in moments of praise and despair. May I sincerely reach out to those you have made. May I love with your love.

58

Cleared for Takeoff

I run in the path of your commands,
for you have broadened my understanding.

PSALM 119:32

When I wait for the airplane to leave the runway, I get anxious. What are they doing? What are they checking? Is the plane okay? Will I ever get to where I want to go? The peace comes after we are cleared for takeoff, and I rest easy when I am free to reach my destination.

Lord, while I wait for things to happen in my life, I get anxious. What are you doing? What will happen? Should I be checking that path instead of this one? My worries well up inside. The doubts begin. But then you clear the path with your commands and your will. The ride could still be bumpy, but the peace is within me. And no matter the destination, my heart is set free.

Protector

The peace of God, which transcends all understanding,
will guard your hearts and your minds in Christ Jesus.

PHILIPPIANS 4:7

am fragile, Lord. When I spend time alone and begin
to think through everything in my life, my guard
comes down. In your presence I reveal my fears and
my hopes. You receive them and shape them into my
future, and I feel comfort.

Even if I don't understand all there is to know
about your ways, I do understand the peace that comes
over me when I give myself to you. It is not easy for me
to trust people in my life. And when I do, I do so carefully and with reservation. But, Lord, when I sit before
you, I know you are guarding my heart and mind. You
are my Protector, and I can be me.

60

Like the Wind

He replied, "You of little faith, why are you so afraid?" Then he got up and rebuked the winds and the waves, and it was completely calm. The men were amazed and asked, "What kind of man is this? Even the winds and the waves obey him!"

MATTHEW 8:26-27

Lord, this certain situation I have been mulling over for a while is getting to me. While talking to friends, it was still in the back of my mind. It sits there and takes up space. Soon it is all I can think about. Lord, you calmed the seas with one command. You cleared the disciples' fears and worries with the mention of peace.

God, I want to be like the winds and waves that obey your word. I want to release the tossing and turning of my concerns over to your power. Give me the peace of a sea that knows the voice of its Creator.

61

Easy

> LORD, *you establish peace for us;*
> *all that we have accomplished you have done for us.*
>
> ISAIAH 26:12

You make my way easy, Lord. I praise you for all that you have done for me and for those I love. Every step of accomplishment in my life is taken on your strength and with your guidance. When I am not in line with what you want for my life, you are there to see me through when I am willing to give up control.

God, you are mighty and gracious. I know that my part of this relationship is easy when compared to all that you do. You create life, and then you give it to me. It is now my choice to give it back to you. Establish peace in my life and in my heart.

62

From Your Hand

LORD our God, all this abundance that we have
provided for building you a temple for your Holy Name
comes from your hand, and all of it belongs to you.

1 CHRONICLES 29:16

look around me at the blessings I have. Even though there is much I do not have, I know I live with abundance. The home I create and offer up to you through hospitality comes from your hand. The job I do so that I can honor you is only possible because of the talents and strengths you provide.

When I take a step forward, it is because you have given me the strength and the direction and the motivation. You inspire all that I do. May my spirit of thanksgiving honor you and return a bit of what you have given to me.

63

Surrounded by Your Plenty

They feast on the abundance of your house;
you give them drink from your river of delights.
For with you is the fountain of life;
in your light we see light.

PSALM 36:8-9

You have called me to sit at a table of plenty, Lord. This feast you present is a life of possibilities and love and growth. The banquet is never-ending, and I stay in your beautiful home not as a guest, but as a family member, a child of your own. Here the cup is filled with your life-giving sacrifice and the plate overflows with food for the spirit and soul.

I may face difficulties in this lifetime, and I may even question why I am allowed to sit at this table of abundance, but I know that this gathering of delights is just a glimpse of eternity's joy.

64

Replenish My Spirit

I will refresh the weary and satisfy the faint.
JEREMIAH 31:25

May your love rain down on me and refresh my spirit. I open my heart as an empty vessel waiting to be filled by your abundant grace. For a time I hid from such expressions of your love. I ran for shelter that did not protect me, but prevented me from encountering your grace. Even then I knew how powerful it would be to share in your bountiful mercy.

Lord, thank you for hearing my prayers over the years, and especially in recent days. I have felt a shift in my heart. I know I am closer to you. It is with deep gratitude that I look ahead and realize that your spiritual abundance will shower down on me when I call upon your mighty, merciful name.

65

Telling of Your Goodness

They will tell of the power of your awesome works—
and I will proclaim your great deeds.
They will celebrate your abundant goodness
and joyfully sing of your righteousness.

PSALM 145:6-7

Lord, your awesome works are everywhere. Your mercy is worthy of celebration and proclamation. Strengthen my spirit so I will be bold when speaking of your greatness. I can be shy about sharing you. Or sometimes it seems self-righteous of me to mention my faith. Guide my heart to speak truth. Let my words flow freely from your love, the Source of all goodness.

Give me a voice to sing of your righteousness. Direct my path toward those who need to hear the good news. When I share about you with others, help them discover and celebrate you. And when I forget to do that in my own life, remind me of this prayer and the praises I feel in my heart today.

66

Reasons

You need to persevere so that when you have done the will of God, you will receive what he has promised.

HEBREWS 10:36

As a child, I asked lots of questions. As your child, those questions still seem to rise in my mind. You'd think I would be past the question "Why?" now that I can research topics, go online, and talk to people who are wise. But my biggest whys relate to life's biggest questions.

When I ask "Why am I here?" or "Why are you asking me to do this?" I know that I have my answer—when I do your will, I am working toward your promises. Those promises from your Word and for my life are my provision and my answer. Right now...that is reason enough.

With or Without

*I know what it is to be in need, and I know what it
is to have plenty. I have learned the secret of being
content in any and every situation, whether well fed
or hungry, whether living in plenty or in want. I can
do everything through him who gives me strength.*

PHILIPPIANS 4:12-13

Lord, your hand has guided me through times of
want and times of plenty. I thank you for being my
Source of strength and guidance. When I hungered for
more and thirsted for opportunity, I followed your way
to brighter days. You guided me through years of abundance so that I could be a devoted steward of my blessings. My status in the world's eyes might change, but
my relationship with you remains the same.

Teach me about contentment, Lord. When I have
material wealth, may I still long for spiritual direction
and nourishment. As I experience difficulties, lead my
thoughts and prayers to you for direction and hope. I
can do all things and survive all circumstances through
your strength.

Dream Come True

*Those who work their land will have abundant food,
but those who chase fantasies have no sense.*

PROVERBS 12:11

have a hard time staying focused. Any bit of dazzle catches my eye. When someone passes by who is living the life I covet, I turn my head and watch them walk away. Fix my mind on the work in front of me, Lord. Return my attention and intentions to the many important and wonderful pieces of my life.

When my head is in the clouds, dreaming of what I want or think I need, pull me back into the abundant day you have given me. I have family, friends, health, and you. The tasks I face today will reap rewards that are real—not just material pleasures, but emotional treasures like satisfaction, fulfillment, contribution, meaning, and purpose. I'll keep dreaming, Lord, but I will ground my days in my dream come true: your unconditional love.

What's Mine Is Yours

What shall I return to the Lord
for all his goodness to me?

Psalm 116:12

Everything I create, Lord, is your creation. My best ideas are manna from heaven. The life I am building is a temple that belongs to you. May I give you all and understand that you are the Source of every good thing I have. When I sit back and look fondly at my family, I know they are a gift from you.

Free me from the burden of owning things, Lord. I will keep up my responsibilities and tend to whatever is in my care, but release me from the desire to claim things as my own: I want. I need. I must have. This train of thought is getting old. I want to rest in knowing you own all things. Blessings come from your hand, and that is where I in turn will place them.

70

Daily Bread

Give us today our daily bread.

Matthew 6:11

Lord, I give you my entire day. I humbly lift up the sacrifice of my daily living to be used to your glory. This empty vessel will be filled with strength, courage, hope, and blessing…your provision flows like living water, and it is plentiful. May others see that you are the One who gives me life and who provides for my daily needs. You, who are the bread of life, do not let any one of your children go hungry.

Where there was nothing in my life, there is now a bounty of goodness. Dry land has turned to thriving pastures. And when I grow hard toward such blessing and cry out for more in the presence of so much, remind me that the daily bread you give is enough. Let my heart open up to your gracious gifts. And may each day I give to you be worthy in your sight.

71

Refreshment

You gave abundant showers, O God;
you refreshed your weary inheritance.
Your people settled in it,
and from your bounty, God, you provided for the poor.

PSALM 68:9-10

grow weary on my journey sometimes. You have carried me often, Lord. I have felt used and useless when going through a rough spot—a dry existence that lacks nourishment and substance. Anything I try to grow just withers and blows away toward the horizon…far away from me.

I look back on these times of my journey. You have sent many showers of refreshment—opportunities appeared when I doubted their existence, kindness humbled me and my bad attitude, and abundant love flooded through me. Your provision has brought me back to life. My path continues, and I am no longer afraid of the droughts I may face along the way.

What a Life Produces

*Our people must learn to devote themselves
to doing what is good, in order to provide for
urgent needs and not live unproductive lives.*

TITUS 3:14

I have been devoted to a number of things over the years. Sadly, a few of them were passing fancies, trendy needs. And I learned a lot from their demise. Lord, you are my one true devotion. Help me take the next step after loving you: following you.

Cultivate in me a character of decency. Let me work hard and carry out deeds of kindness. May your seeds of grace fall on fertile soil in my heart so a harvest of honor is later reaped. I pray that I would turn your provision into continuous seasons of productive goodness. I want to live a life pleasing to you and beneficial to others. Direct me in your ways and keep my spirit burning with devotion.

Lending a Hand

*She opens her arms to the poor
and extends her hands to the needy.*

PROVERBS 31:20

To whom should I give today? Whom can I help? Let me start the day with this question, Lord. If I am asking to be of service, then I cannot ignore the opportunities when they arise. I have looked into needy faces and kept walking. I think too much about such things. My mind asks, "How can I fix someone's life?"

You ask me to be a woman of charity and kindness. My actions to assist another child of God become a part of your will for that person. You are not calling me to fix her, to make her whole. Only you can do that. My job is to lend a hand along the way.

74

The Riches of Hope

*Command those who are rich in this present world
not to be arrogant nor to put their hope in wealth,
which is so uncertain, but to put their hope in
God, who richly provides us with everything for our
enjoyment. Command them to do good, to be rich in
good deeds, and to be generous and willing to share.*

1 TIMOTHY 6:17-18

You are my Provider, Lord. You gave me life, and you will create ways for me to follow in your way. I should not question this, yet I have been in situations where financial uncertainty caused me to doubt the plans you have for me. I question what tomorrow might bring, rather than counting on what my Lord might bring.

I turn my circumstances over to you today. I will accept the goodness and the riches you allow. From the blessings you give, I will give to other people. I will strive to put my hope in you, God, not in my bank account. Let this step of faith encourage me to take bigger leaps tomorrow.

75

All Blessings Flow

*You will be made rich in every way so that you can
be generous on every occasion, and through us your
generosity will result in thanksgiving to God.*

2 CORINTHIANS 9:11

The riches I can claim are yours. They should flow
through me and on to other people as you see fit.
Lord, help me work through the urge to hold on to
wealth. My fear of the future and my perceived need
turn my willingness into reluctance. Keep me from
blocking the blessings you have for other people.

Give me personal contact with those who need provision, or let me hear of a specific need I can help fill.
My obedience can turn another person's cry for help
into songs of thanksgiving.

76

Pure Refreshment

A generous person will prosper;
whoever refreshes others will be refreshed.

PROVERBS 11:25

God, I have so much. Show me how to share the nonmonetary blessings I have: family, health, opportunity, stability, shelter, friends. Maybe I could invite someone to a family gathering during the holidays. I could encourage a friend with handwritten notes. I could use my health and participate in a fundraiser walk. There are so many ways for me to extend your provision to other people.

Refresh me, Lord. Fill me with the joy of giving.

And let each offering refresh the spirit of another.

77

The Reluctant Servant

The precepts of the LORD are right,
giving joy to the heart.

PSALM 19:8

Lord, when I was a child, I hated being told what to do. If asked to perform a chore, I resisted, found distractions, or muddled my way through it. Guidelines felt like punishment. I knew I was capable of doing the things that were asked of me—I just wanted to do them in my own way. I gave of myself in my own time frame. How often do I resist your precepts, Lord? I see the right way to give or serve, yet I fight it. I don't want to change my plans or be inconvenienced. I have had a reluctant heart, Lord, and I am sorry. Help me to follow your commands with a giving spirit. I have asked many times before, but I still long to have a joyful heart that follows your way.

78

Giving Light

God said, "Let there be lights in the vault of the sky to separate the day from the night, and let them serve as signs to mark sacred times, and days and years, and let them be lights in the vault of the sky to give light on the earth."

GENESIS 1:14-15

Some people light up a room. I know Christians who reflect your radiance everywhere they go, Lord. I want this kind of radiance in my life. My hope is to have a faith that is a light in the darkness of despair and indifference.

Guide me into action, Lord. Don't let me fall into a dark pit of apathy and make a home there. The further I distance myself from your light, the less likely I am to be reignited in my passion for your will. Most of all, I want my hope in you to offer light on the earth. Help me shine, Lord.

79

Private Donations

*When you give to the needy, do not let your left hand
know what your right hand is doing, so that your
giving may be in secret. Then your Father, who
sees what is done in secret, will reward you.*

MATTHEW 6:3-4

It is hard to resist taking credit, Lord. Truth is, I am taking credit away from you every time I seek acknowledgment for giving my time, energy, or money. I feel so utterly human when I want affirmation. Isn't it enough to know that you see me and are pleased? Lord, help me to desire heaven's praise above all else. Guard me from a pretentious existence that feeds off recognition or success.

Any time I reach out to give to another, I am giving from your source of plenty, not from any abundance I have created on my own. The credit is yours to have. Humble my spirit so that the blessing of giving resides in my heart—in secret, under your proud gaze. Pleasing you, Lord, is the only reward I desire.

80

Praise You

*Speak to one another with psalms, hymns, and songs
from the Spirit. Sing and make music from your heart
to the Lord, always giving thanks to God the Father
for everything, in the name of our Lord Jesus Christ.*

EPHESIANS 5:19-20

Praise you. My spirits are lifted just saying that to you. So why am I quick to squelch the music of my soul? Some time ago, I told myself that songs and praises were shallow and emotional. Forgive me, Lord. I have forgotten that rejoicing is not frivolity—it is an offering to you.

I have held my tongue for too long. I will raise my hands to the sky. I will lift my voice to the heavens, and I will give you praise, Lord, for you are worthy. Hear my hymn of thanksgiving, Lord, for all you have done and are doing in my life. I will not silence my spirit in your presence again.

81

Ready to Believe

Jesus replied, "Truly I tell you, if you have faith and do not doubt, not only can you do what was done to the fig tree, but also you can say to this mountain, 'Go, throw yourself into the sea,' and it will be done. If you believe, you will receive whatever you ask for in prayer."

MATTHEW 21:21-22

My prayers don't always reflect a faith of true believing, Lord. I find myself asking without faith in the outcome, without fully trusting that you are listening. Fill my heart with faith that leaves no room for doubt. Let my questions be those of a seeker desiring a deeper relationship with you, rather than those of a person who places obstacles between my life and the One who made it.

As I practice the discipline of prayer, may it make me ready to receive all that is good, holy, and of you. May my lips never release words that are not lifted up in faith.

82

Receive Me

Take words with you and return to the LORD.
Say to him: "Forgive all our sins and receive us
graciously, that we may offer the fruit of our lips."

HOSEA 14:2

Receive me, Lord. Take my enthusiasm, my questions, my willingness, and shape them into someone who seeks only what is of you and from your hand. Receive my efforts and clean away the sin that can taint the good things that come from my life.

Receive my words, hear them within your sweet grace so that they are pleasing to you. May my expressed thoughts and prayers be my promise of ongoing dialogue. My desire to reach you and to be held in your hand has become a longing. My heart is full as you receive your child's simple words, faltering praises, and pleading inquiries.

83

The Whole Me

Do not reject me or forsake me, God my Savior.
Though my father and mother forsake me,
the LORD will receive me.
Teach me your way, LORD;
lead me in a straight path because of my oppressors.

PSALM 27:9-11

There are times when people in my life do not understand me. Or maybe they see only a part of me, rather than the whole. This has occurred so many times that I thought it was the only way to be viewed...in pieces. But Lord, you receive me as a whole being. You see the good, the bad, and the desire to do right.

I expect a lot out of people, those close to me and even those I just happen to meet. Help me to understand that even if they let me down or forsake that part of me that they know, this does not define my life. This does not keep me from the path you have laid out before me. I pray to become the whole person you created me to be so that you will receive me with joy.

84

Accept My Praise

Accept, LORD, the willing praise of my mouth,
and teach me your laws.

PSALM 119:108

Do you look at the way I live out my faith and consider my praise worthy of your attention, Lord? Are my prayers of praise acceptable offerings? I do not always know what to say to honor all that you are. Search my heart to discover the depth of my love and gratitude. May what you find be pleasing.

Though it can take me a while to get through my prayers to my praises, Lord, they are willing offerings and reflect the spirit I aspire to have every waking moment.

You Know Me

LORD, you understand;
remember me and care for me.

JEREMIAH 15:15

You see me when nobody else does. You know me when nobody else inquires. You see me when others look past me. You care for me when others are too busy. Being your child means I am nourished spiritually and emotionally even when I feel alone.

How many times have I looked to others to feed me my sense of value? God, renew my strength and my understanding of how much you care. I am known by the Creator of the universe, and he loves me!

86

Strange Food

*He humbled you, causing you to hunger and
then feeding you with manna, which neither you
nor your fathers had known, to teach you that
man does not live on bread alone but on every
word that comes from the mouth of the LORD.*

DEUTERONOMY 8:3

have begged for assistance and for you to ease my hunger, Lord. There is so much that I want. My journey is difficult at times, and I seek support. I have asked over and over for you to send answers and understanding and help.

Lord, all this time you've been providing me with all that I need. My concerns are understood. My path might not look like I want it to, but you are paving it with your promises. Your Word and these promises are different than the food I asked for, but they nourish me and renew my spirit.

87

Casting Cares

Cast your cares on the LORD
and he will sustain you.

PSALM 55:22

What do people do when they don't have you in their lives? Some nights I lie awake wondering where I would be if I hadn't met you. I am blessed with strong relationships and friendships, yet not one person in my life could handle the cares and worries I entrust to you.

Not only do you hear my troubles, but you exchange them for what I need in that moment and for the long journey. People provide pat answers; you provide eternal promises. I am grateful to bring my whole heart to you.

88

Source of Life

You care for the land and water it;
you enrich it abundantly.

PSALM 65:9

Showers cleanse the air. Sun warms the soil. Winds blow seeds across the land. Seasons set in motion by your hand nourish the plants and the people and the generations of those who live beneath your gaze.

My life feels like a complete system—a mini-world—that depends on your cleansing grace, the warmth of your compassion, and your transforming love. Help me harvest the seeds you have planted in my soul. I know that abundance awaits me.

Receiving God's Blessing

May God give you heaven's dew and earth's
richness—an abundance of grain and new wine.

GENESIS 27:28

have had my share of goodness, Lord. I need only to
look at my immediate surroundings and the people in
my life to see how richly I have been blessed. Why do I
pay such close attention to the imperfections of my life?
My job could be more important. My family could be
a bit more agreeable. My body could be in better shape,
like the woman on that television show. My car could
be newer and have all of those extras I saw on the com-
mercials that interrupted that television show. You see
how my mind starts to destroy all the blessings?

Lord, open my eyes to the good in all situations.
Let the times of poverty I experience cause me to
embrace the richness of your bounty. Help me to be
aware of the manna that falls from heaven and lands
in my life.

90

Satisfied by Grace

Out of his fullness we have all received
grace in place of grace already given.

JOHN 1:16

look at the life you have given me, Lord, and I see great blessings. You have provided for my needs. Your grace has allowed me to reach goals. There is so much more I want to do, but I have learned to wait on your timing. There is an order to godly things. When I let your priorities guide my journey, blessings build upon blessings.

Hold me back when I try to force advancement, Lord. I don't want anything in my life, even if it resembles success, if it is not from you. I pray for discernment to know the difference between aspirations fabricated by my heart and those born of your will. Free me from thoughts of envy, judgment, and greed. I want to be satisfied by your grace alone.

91

Inherit a Blessing

Do not repay evil with evil or insult with insult. On the contrary, repay evil with blessing, because to this you were called so that you may inherit a blessing.

1 PETER 3:9

Lord, I am more likely to hold a grudge than release a blessing when someone has hurt me. My reaction to conflict reveals how desperately I need your forgiveness to flow through me. Heal me from the anger that rises so quickly. I want to reflect your image to others, even those who are working against me.

Let me ponder your holiness before facing a potentially difficult encounter or situation. I want to arm myself with your Word, your strength, and your compassion so I can honor your name with my actions. I will inherit a blessing by spreading the legacy of your love.

92

Find Me Righteous

Surely, LORD, you bless the righteous;
you surround them with your favor as with a shield.

PSALM 5:12

Search my heart, O Lord. May you find it righteous and pure. I long for joy in my life. This season of hardship has tempted me to question how your blessings are given. What have I done to deserve this pain? But my heart knows I am forgiven—your mercy covers my sins. How can I use this time to draw closer to you rather than challenge your mercy?

What do you want me to learn from my life today? Alleviate my confusion. Pierce my heart with your love. Encourage me with the security of believing friends. Saturate my days with evidence of blessings yet to come. Surround me with your favor. Protect my fragile heart.

93

Meditating on Truth

Keep me from deceitful ways;
be gracious to me and teach me your law.

PSALM 119:29

When I think about how much time I have spent in my life meditating on half-truths and falsehoods instead of on your way, it makes me tired. I used all my energy trying to second-guess every good thing in my life. I got used to not trusting any situation or person…or even you. I pray for your protection, Lord. Keep me in the truth of your laws. I want to trust your way without hesitation.

As I walk in your truth and seek it with longing and intention, I will only meditate on that which is from you and of you. Keep me from the edge of doubt so that I do not follow the path of false teachings and waste more precious time.

94

Been There

Though you have made me see troubles,
many and bitter, you will restore my life again;
from the depths of the earth you will again bring me up.
You will increase my honor and comfort me once more.

PSALM 71:20-21

The beauty of having been there in the hard times is that I have been there during the good times and the moments of redemption that follow. Lord, I trust you with my life, and I am beginning to release other people to your care as well. By following your way and trusting you to restore me to a new creation, I can bring honor to you.

There is great comfort in knowing I have a place to turn. I do not know how other people grow to trust the way life unfolds. I place my hope in that which is sure and true. I give my heart, my life to you.

95

Modeled Faith

*We ought always to thank God for you, brothers
and sisters loved by the Lord, because God chose
you as firstfruits to be saved through the sanctifying
work of the Spirit and through belief in the truth.*

2 THESSALONIANS 2:13

God, thank you for the people in my life who offer me safe places and safe relationships that show me how to trust. Their adherence to what is true and noble and honorable inspires me to live a godly life. When I watch the Holy Spirit leading the decisions and acts of other people, I do see how your power works through each person and circumstance.

Lord, help me trust you and your Spirit just as the faithful followers do. Fill me with the same courage and willingness to be obedient to your calling and your will. I have entrusted my eternity to you. May I learn to entrust my present moment, my now, to you as well.

96

Entrusting It All

In you, LORD my God, I put my trust.
PSALM 25:1

Lord, you see how I struggle with sharing parts of myself with other people. I hold on to bits and pieces of my life to preserve it. I am reluctant to learn that in order to create a bond of trust, I need to give to people. But in my spiritual life I desperately want to learn how to give myself over to you. My soul longs to be in your possession.

Lord, please see beyond my stubborn ways of self-protection to the heart that does beat for you. Today I will give you more of myself than ever before. I will trust you with my decisions, my relationships, my concerns, and my future.

Relying on You

Pay attention and turn your ear to the sayings of the wise;
apply your heart to what I teach, for it is pleasing
when you keep them in your heart and have all
of them ready on your lips. So that your trust may
be in the LORD, I teach you today, even you.

PROVERBS 22:17-19

Trusting in you changes everything, Lord. I will not dwell on past failings, and I won't wager on things to come. Because right now is my most important time frame. Help me to seek your ways more earnestly. Let my thoughts and my actions be pure in your sight, Lord. I will heed the lessons of the wise.

I see the day ahead and imagine ways to improve. I will look for people who need encouragement, including myself, and will recite words of your faithfulness. I will watch for the opportunities and unique moments you offer that teach me more about you. Yes, I told myself yesterday I was not worthy of your love…but the assurance of the sunrise this morning spoke of your grace. I trust you, Lord.

A Song to Sing

I trust in your unfailing love;
my heart rejoices in your salvation.
I will sing the LORD's praise, for he has been good to me.

PSALM 13:5-6

God, you have been so good to me. I trust you and what you are doing in my life. Some days I clearly see your love for me. I received a kind word at a time of sorrow. I was offered help when I was afraid to ask. And just when I thought I could not continue, I had a vision of what your hand was doing in that very circumstance. I could not navigate my days without trusting your love and intent for good. I pray that my actions translate into lyrics for the world to hear. I want everyone to know the song of your love and mercy. I lift up my voice to proclaim your goodness. "I know a love that never fails me!" I cry out into a world of people who know only of broken love and misplaced trust. Thank you, Lord, for giving me a song to sing.

You Are Mine

I trust in you, LORD;
I say, "You are my God."

PSALM 31:14

Lord, I want my lips to praise you in all situations. No matter the circumstances I am in, I want my first thoughts to be of praise, because I trust you with my life. May everything I do be a witness to this trust. When people around me attempt to fix my problems with temporal solutions, I will stand firm in my belief. How often do I say, "You are my God"? Do my actions speak this? Do my relationships reflect this truth? I want every part of my life to resound with this statement. When your peace replaces my worry, I want others to hear the reason. Let it be clear to people I meet that my trust is placed only in you. Help me to say it loudly, even in the silent moments that follow difficult times.

Entrusting a Soul

As for me, I trust in you.
PSALM 55:23

In a moment of possible failure, Lord, am I trusting you to save me—or to save face for me? Help me lift up my soul without requirements and requests. I trust you to work out this situation for good, not evil. My humanity begs me to avoid humiliation at all costs, but I know I will be saved for different reasons: My weakness becomes evidence of your strength. My destruction turns into a testimony of your instruction and mercy.

Do not let me shame you, Lord. Let this moment shine light upon your goodness. May it cast shadows on my need for recognition or reputation. Please accept this offering of my soul. There are no strings attached—only complete trust and gratitude come with this sacrifice.

101

Lighting the Way

Your word is a lamp for my feet,
a light on my path.

PSALM 119:105

I'm beginning to see how your Word is my source of light and wisdom to get through my days. It reveals the pitfalls and the peaks, and it guides my every step. When I try to use my limited knowledge and understanding to make my way forward, I realize it is like bringing my flashlight to camp in the middle of nowhere. I'm prepared. Ready. Certain my offering will make a difference. And then your moon rises. Your stars come out. I put away my poor substitution that was never needed. You illuminate the road ahead.

The world has so few light sources. Thank you, Lord, for being my lamp, my sun, my inner light, and the light unto the world.

102

As Sure as the Sun

Let us acknowledge the LORD;
let us press on to acknowledge him.
As surely as the sun rises, he will appear;
he will come to us like the winter rains,
like the spring rains that water the earth.

HOSEA 6:3

awaken each day with the certainty that I will be greeted by the dawn. I welcome the joys and the challenges ahead. And with each day, you offer the certainty of fellowship and renewal—I just need to acknowledge and trust your truths.

Shower me with blessings, circumstances for growth, and opportunities to know you better. You come like the rains and the sunshine into my life to refresh and nourish me. I praise you.

103

Should I?

*Commit to the Lord whatever you do,
and he will establish your plans.*

PROVERBS 16:3

Should I, Lord? I've been thinking about a certain decision lately, but it would involve trusting you completely. You know how reserved I've been about such things—is this the time for me to take the plunge? I try to do so much on my own. I have even prided myself on this acquired skill. But when I have success, is it really what you wanted for me? And if I fail, is it because I have not listened to you?

Commitment is a scary word and an even scarier action. Help me trust you, Lord. Where there is doubt, fill me with your confidence. I want to succeed in faith.

104

Dwelling Place

*Trust in the L*ORD *and do good;*
dwell in the land and enjoy safe pasture.
*Take delight in the L*ORD
and he will give you the desires of your heart.

PSALM 37:3-4

I might move five, six times in my life, or more…but my home is always with you, Lord. Over the years you have shown me time after time how faithful you are to those who trust you. My insecurities lead me astray, but my faith always returns me to your presence.

My delight is in you and your goodness. Teach me to trust your purposes for my life and shape the desires of my heart to fulfill your perfect will.

I'm Pouting

These people have stubborn and rebellious hearts;
they have turned aside and gone away.

JEREMIAH 5:23

won't. I won't, Lord. Not just yet. I know I should let go of my recent behavior, but I just don't feel ready. You could make me, but you choose not to. Now, my choice is to pout for a while. My fingers are turning white as I grip this thing I will not release to you. When did I become so difficult?

Sure, I'm shaking a little bit. I am growing weary. This is, after all, a heavy burden. I think I'll set it down for a minute…just long enough to get sustenance. What a relief to not have that weight dragging me down. I sure feel better, Lord. I'm picking it up again— this time to hand it over to you, Lord. I get it…when I let go of such things, I am free. I am choosing to be free, Lord. Thank you for waiting.

106

Come Near to Me, Lord

Submit yourselves, then, to God.
Resist the devil, and he will flee from you.
Come near to God and he will come near to you.

JAMES 4:7-8

Submission is one of those concepts that bothers me, Lord. If you must know, it causes me to feel quite threatened. Help me to see the security that follows submission. I want to be under your authority, your control, your cover of love. Forgive me for being tied to my identity as a self-made person. I have strived so long for control of my life that it feels unnatural to give it over to you.

Release me from my fear of submission, Lord. It has created a wall between us. Please come near to me. Empower me with the strength to resist the temptation to remain in control. I look forward to claiming the identity of a God-made person.

I Am Your Child

The living, the living—they praise you, as I am doing
today; fathers tell their children about your faithfulness.

ISAIAH 38:19

Lord, I live today as your child. I plan to focus on this identity. Undoubtedly I will be asking for guidance, messing things up, getting your pristine plans dirty, and constantly asking, "Why? Why?" But you are used to the floundering of your children. You are a patient parent. The lessons you have taught me in your Word and through your active love are helping me grow. I can see the person you want me to become.

Like a child, I will run in different directions before asking the way. And by then, I will probably need to be carried. It is very exhausting being a child. But now, as you lift me up and comfort me with your promise of love and grace, I settle down. To be wrapped in your faithfulness is all I needed…I just didn't know how to get there. When I am done resting, will you tell me a story? I love the one about the day I became your child.

108

Finding My Way Home

Love and faithfulness meet together;
righteousness and peace kiss each other.
Faithfulness springs forth from the earth,
and righteousness looks down from heaven.

PSALM 85:10-11

At the intersection of your love and faithfulness, Lord, I have found my life. For years I have taken many detours. My soul longed for intrigue, so it turned down curious, narrow avenues; I found only pain and suffering. My spirit craved success and celebrity, so I ventured along the flashy main streets, only to find failure and isolation.

Then I stopped following my "wants" and listened to my heart. My pace quickened as I caught a glimpse of the crossroads ahead. You waited patiently for me on the corner. I didn't ask what it was you were promising or how long it would last. I could see home in your eyes, and it went on forever.

Flawless and Faithful

LORD, you are my God;
I will exalt you and praise your name,
for in perfect faithfulness you have done
wonderful things, things planned long ago.

ISAIAH 25:1

I did not give you much to work with early on in my life, Lord. What a sight I was back then. Rumpled, tough, stubborn, and ignorant. "Just try to do something with this!" I challenged you on a particularly bad day. I was acting out the courage found in movie heroes, but my heart was really pleading with you, "Please—do something with my life."

You answered this cry for help because you knew I would someday step into your faithfulness and be transformed into a shining, perfect child of God. You turned my spirit of spite into a heart of praise. Praise you, Lord. Long ago you planned such wonderful things for my life. I cannot wait to see where your faithfulness will lead.

110

Your Creation Endures

*Your faithfulness continues through all generations;
you established the earth, and it endures.*

PSALM 119:90

Beneath my feet is proof of your commitment, Lord. You established the earth and set it in motion to serve your children and your greater purpose. Your creation speaks of your enduring faithfulness. God, the lineage of just one family has countless testimonies of your limitless love.

I pray that I will carry on stories of your holiness to others in my family. Let my praises spread to those in my spiritual family. May I then speak of your goodness to those who do not yet know you. May I always be a faithful child who models the faithfulness of my Father.

| | |

Communication Then and Now

*In the past God spoke to our ancestors through
the prophets at many times and in various ways,
but in these last days he has spoken to us by his
Son, whom he appointed heir of all things, and
through whom also he made the universe.*

HEBREWS 1:1-2

God, you had a communication plan in place at the inception of the universe. You knew your children would need to hear your voice. There are times I wish that your prophets were still so easily recognized. Yet, would I even listen in this day and age? Likely, I'd bustle right past a proclaimed prophet in my hurry to catch the subway.

Lord, you know the shape of the past and the shape of things to come. You saw that the world would need a relationship with your Son. A personal Savior to wake us up from our blurry, busy lives. I see you, God. I hear you. And I thank you for keeping the line of communication open through the power of your Son.

112

Hope for the Future

*Everything that was written in the past was
written to teach us, so that through endurance
taught in the Scriptures and the encouragement
they provide we might have hope.*

ROMANS 15:4

Lord, the wisdom of the lessons found in your Word speaks to my life today. I thank you for the fresh hope that breathes through words scribed so many years ago. I am amazed how Scripture moves me. Some people try to cast it away as irrelevant, but they have not immersed themselves in your truths.

You care so much for me that you created an unending source of encouragement and instruction. Help me to stay grounded in the teachings of the Bible, Lord. Show me the opportunities to live out the lessons of Scripture. I want to be an active student of your love and your ways.

The Rains Are Over

See! The winter is past; the rains are over and gone.
Flowers appear on the earth;
the season of singing has come.

SONG OF SOLOMON 2:11-12

Days of hardship and pain have rained down in my past, Lord. There were storms that destroyed the foundations I had built. Floods swept away the hope I had placed in material things and in the strength I thought I saw in others. All that remained was the washed-out land of disappointment. But that was in the past. A time when I could not see a future.

Now the flowers sprout and shout from the earth. They sing a song of your faithfulness. This is a new season for me, Lord. Past sorrows fade away and future hopes and dreams grow strong. You offer me this renewal every day, Lord. I am grateful for the rains, for they have prepared my soul to receive the blessings.

114

Moving On

Forget the former things;
do not dwell on the past.
See, I am doing a new thing!
Now it springs up; do you not perceive it?

ISAIAH 43:18-19

Free me from the past, Lord. I spend too much time there. Good times that have come and gone replay in my mind so often that I miss the wonder of today's joy. Cause me to return to the present, Lord. Draw my attention back to the life in front of me. My past has nothing to offer you or myself. But today...now...has so much to offer.

Give me a view of new wonders you are doing. I imagine they are brilliant happenings. Do not let my mind slip to the past, except to count the times you have blessed me. Then I must move on. My past serves my future...it is a foundation for all days that follow. Now, I must invest my time, my dreams, my prayers on the future you have carved out for me.

Restored by Faith

He touched their eyes and said, "According to your faith will it be done to you"; and their sight was restored.

MATTHEW 9:29-30

Heal me, Lord, from the inside out. My spirit is sick from worry and stress. Create a healthy soul inside this temple. I have neglected to nourish my spirit—show me the way back. Wounds ignored for too long need your healing touch. Remove scars that remind me of old but not forgotten hurts. I trust you to mend my brokenness.

Let me have the same belief when I need physical healing. I know you hear and answer these prayers. Help me to understand that I do not understand the vast number of ways in which you heal. My human eyes can be blind to your acts of mercy. Restore my sight, Lord. Let me feel your touch and hear you say, "According to your faith will it be done to you."

116

Facing the Storm

Suddenly a furious storm came up on the lake, so that the waves swept over the boat. But Jesus was sleeping. The disciples went and woke him, saying, "Lord, save us! We're going to drown!" He replied, "You of little faith, why are you so afraid?" Then he got up and rebuked the winds and the waves, and it was completely calm.

MATTHEW 8:24-26

Craziness consumes me, Lord. Beneath the confidence I show the world, God, you know an ocean of fear rocks and swells. I feel it when I spend a few minutes in silence. That's why I avoid quiet time with you. I'm afraid to face the storm.

God, I am like the disciples who followed you and listened to your explanations of what it means to believe. I've witnessed your faithfulness, yet I cry, "Save me," with little faith. Pull my gaze to your eyes and away from the waves about to crash into my ordered world. When the winds die down and I face you on the calm waters, I want to be found standing as a believer.

Nothing Is Impossible

*Truly I tell you, if you have faith as small as a
mustard seed, you can say to this mountain,
"Move from here to there," and it will move.
Nothing will be impossible for you.*

MATTHEW 17:20

All-powerful Lord, your might is a part of my life.
The incredibleness of this truth is my reason for
often neglecting your resource. How can it be possible
that you allow your children such strength? What an
awesome God you are. History shows us that kings of
men often strip their followers of hope. But you clothe
those in your kingdom with possibility.

Show me what faith, even the smallest faith, can
accomplish, Lord. Next time I face a mountain on my
spiritual journey, I will not ask if you will help me to
the top. Instead, I will draw forth a faith that requires
the obstacle be moved altogether.

118

Promises to Others

Do we not all have one Father? Did not one God
create us? Why do we profane the covenant of our
fathers by being unfaithful to one another?

MALACHI 2:10

want to be a keeper of promises. Lord, lead me to make only commitments I am strong enough to fulfill. Good intentions cause me to step up to meet many needs. But I have discovered something...I am not a good judge of time and responsibility. Forgive me for letting down even one other person. Free in your mercy, I do not have to live a life buried in guilt—but I do desire to be honorable before others and you.

Guard me from becoming overconfident and independent. That is when I take on too many demands. Protect me from breaking bread with a friend one day, then breaking faith with them on another. Bless me with a heart whose generosity is followed by perseverance and commitment.

The Life of Belief

*Through him you believe in God, who raised
him from the dead and glorified him, and
so your faith and hope are in God.*

1 PETER 1:21

When I embraced belief and experienced your everlasting love, I had no idea how much I would need you. But you did. You knew the hurts and the difficulties I would face. My faith in you has given me a new life. I still face trials that bring me to my knees, but now I can rejoice in the ways your power of resurrection is evident in my life. My change of heart, the transformation of my thoughts, and a reimagining of my purpose to name a few.

May "believer" never be a label but a way of life. A way of seeing, experiencing my days, relationships, and the holiness of everyday moments. I am always grateful to have faith in you, God, but it is on days when I feel discouraged that I celebrate your strength all the more.

120

Yes, Lord

*When he had gone indoors, the blind men came
to him, and he asked them, "Do you believe that
I am able to do this?" "Yes, Lord," they replied.*

MATTHEW 9:28

will just say it, Lord. A desire of my heart is to have more people in my life whom I love and who love me. I try not to think about it too much because I don't want to miss out on the goodness of the life I do have. Show me how to expand my heart, be vulnerable, and to express the hospitality of your heart. Open my eyes so I can see those people you bring into my life. You give me many people to care about and build up.

Today, I pray for your leading in the area of love. I say, "Yes, Lord, I believe." I believe you are able to open my eyes to the possibility of more love. Help me rest in the truth that my identity is not based on my marital status but on my belief in you.

121

Tossing and Turning

*If any of you lacks wisdom, you should ask God, who
gives generously to all without finding fault, and it
will be given to you. But when you ask, you must
believe and not doubt, because the one who doubts is
like a wave of the sea, blown and tossed by the wind.*

JAMES 1:5-6

I spent another sleepless night because of worries that plagued my every thought. The moment I surfaced, my anxieties squelched my peace. My tossing and turning became physical and spiritual. Lord, I want to have the kind of belief that releases my concerns to your care. Right now I keep watch over my problems like I am the one in control.

Free me of this micromanagement of my life. I have faith that you will tend to my needs as the Shepherd who loves his flock. Even when I don't know how tomorrow will turn out, I have peace in you.

122

Do I Have That?

Jesus turned and saw her. "Take heart, daughter,"
he said, "your faith has healed you." And
the woman was healed at that moment.

MATTHEW 9:22

think of the woman you healed, Lord. You called her daughter and said her faith healed her. Do I have that kind of faith, Lord? I know that you hear the cries of my heart and mend the broken places of my spirit. But when I reach out to touch the hem of your garment, do I have the kind of faith that changes things?

Lord, I leave my path up to you. Each day I try to have more faith. But in the moments when it is difficult for me to reach out, please give me the belief I need. I long to hear you call me your child.

123

Alone with the Lord

*We live by faith, not by sight. We are confident,
I say, and would prefer to be away from
the body and at home with the Lord.*

2 CORINTHIANS 5:7-8

As soon as I step away from the conversations with others, the distractions, and the busyness, my heart's first impulse is to run to you. When I am alone and experiencing solitude, I am also experiencing your presence with more intensity.

During times of aloneness, my faith in you seems clearer, brighter, and stronger. It is because I am leaning on you completely. There is no greater peace than to be at home with you. I have faith that this is a mere echo of what it feels like to go home to heaven.

124

Head for the Hills

*After he had dismissed them, [Jesus] went up
on a mountainside by himself to pray. When
evening came, he was there alone.*

MATTHEW 14:23

I am following your lead, Lord. I get it now more than ever. Your most difficult times were covered and followed with prayer. After long days of praying over others and healing them, you still yearned to pray to your Father.

There is so much going on in my life. Good things. Hard things. Some things that I have yet to figure out. I am learning to bring all to you in prayer and to seek your face no matter the circumstances. It is time to unwind, but my heart is heading for the hills to spend moments of solitude with its Maker.

125

Hear My Cries

*Evening, morning and noon
I cry out in distress,
and he hears my voice.*

PSALM 55:17

I am like an infant who needs comfort, food, and reassurance around the clock. I cry out to you in the morning when I am pondering what questions the day might present. I seek to connect with you when the day is going full speed and I need a right perspective to survive. In the evening, my cries are even greater. I need to know that you are with me even as distractions fall away and I am left vulnerable and silent. Hear my cries, Abba Father.

126

Only You

Truly my soul finds rest in God;
my salvation comes from him.

PSALM 62:1

Lord, when you look at my past, does it hurt you to see the many times I tried to save myself? Or when I asked others to save me? I avoided being alone with you because I wasn't ready to exchange my version of salvation for yours. I didn't believe I was worth the grace.

Solitude no longer scares me. I welcome it because my soul rests in your hands. I don't want to find this comfort anywhere else. Only you can save me. Only now can I see that your love makes me worthy.

127

The Luxury of Time

*Very early in the morning, while it was still
dark, Jesus got up, left the house and went
off to a solitary place, where he prayed.*

MARK 1:35

God, my life is filled with incredible blessings, but often I am too bothered by small things to notice these gifts. My friends complain that they rarely get a moment to themselves. My coworkers, who put in overtime, long for a vacation. Parents of kids of all ages feel pulled in 20 directions. No matter what life situation a person has, the sense of time passing quickly can become overwhelming. We all need to breathe and find our way back to your presence.

Reveal to me the wonders of time spent in solitude. Give me the peace of spirit to enjoy what I have. Allow my thoughts to wind down and settle on you. Time is a squandered luxury when I don't pay attention. Time is a blessing when I place my attention on you.

128

Family Portrait

God sets the lonely in families.
PSALM 68:6

There have been times when I have waited on you to make introductions to those who will become my people, my community. Thank you, God, for placing me in a family of friends, relatives, coworkers, and neighbors. I need only to look around me to see that family can be and mean so many different things. When I need help with a project, I know who to call. When I want someone to pray for me, I have those people too.

Lord, help me find comfort in you and in those you place in my life. You have set me among those willing to reach out. Move me from loneliness to belonging. And when I feel disconnected, remind me to look again at people who fill my life…remind me to look at the family portrait you orchestrated.

129

You Alone

He alone is my rock and my salvation;
he is my fortress, I will never be shaken.

PSALM 62:2

You are my rock, my salvation, my strength, and my vision of all that is good and just. Never will this life I build be shaken and destroyed because you are the one who sees me through every battle, every storm, and every harm.

The foundation of faith I build my hopes upon will not be wiped out from beneath me. My trust is in your remarkable power, and not in my own strength. During my times of weakness or sorrow, or when night seems never-ending, I seek you alone, for only you can save me and comfort this heart of mine.

130

When Others Leave

*You will leave me all alone. Yet I am not
alone, for my Father is with me.*

JOHN 16:32

Lord, I might feel alone, but I know your eyes watch over me in my times of solitude and yearning. You guide my steps carefully and with the hands of a loving Father. There is only rest when a person comes to you. In the stillness of a new day, I find my peace here in your tender mercy.

I have had people come and go in my life. Some have disappointed me so much that I still carry the hurt along my journey. Release me from these concerns. My heart sings with the song of truth, and it resounds with the sweetness and sureness of your presence.

131

Hold My Tongue

If you have anything to say, answer me;
speak up, for I want to vindicate you.
But if not, then listen to me;
be silent, and I will teach you wisdom.

JOB 33:32-33

God, I've never asked for this before, but I need to learn to be silent. You have placed wise people in my life who have advice and clear thinking to offer me. My pride gets in the way, and I pretend to know what I am doing. But I want to hear their truths. I want to be open to what you are teaching me through them.

Hold my tongue, open my ears, and prepare my heart for all you are saying to me.

132

Speaking with Actions

*For it is God's will that by doing good you should
silence the ignorant talk of foolish people.*

1 PETER 2:15

As I think over the day, I realize there were many opportunities to express my beliefs through my actions. Lord, help me have a faith so real, so infused throughout my being that I do not have to rely just on words to express my love for you.

When I serve you by being compassionate, wise, generous, forgiving, and loving, those who want to undermine faith with false accusations or ignorant comments will be silenced, and those who long to know more about you will have a chance to "hear" the good news.

133

Tears

My God, I cry out by day, but you do not answer,
by night, but I find no rest.

PSALM 22:2

Lord, do you hear my cries? I am lonely. My thoughts at night seem to echo with my sadness and memories of past disappointments. The distractions of daytime turn my thoughts toward tasks, goals, next steps, and how to respond to what is in front of me; yet, when there is a pause, my mind turns again toward my spiritual aloneness. I want to feel your presence. I want to hear from you; I want to be certain you are right here beside me.

God, listen to the brokenness of my spirit. I pray for comfort as I sit in the silence and welcome the balm of your presence.

134

Turning, Turning

You turned my wailing into dancing;
you removed my sackcloth and clothed me with joy,
that my heart may sing to you and not be silent.

PSALM 30:11-12

My time of weeping has ended. The grieving that once consumed me has dissipated into the night. My heart is turning toward joy and life. My feet are turning as I dance into a new stage.

Oh, how I have waited for you to turn my sorrow to celebration. My lips cannot stop praising you and singing of your goodness. I want to tell the world that you walk with us through the pain and you rejoice with us in our day of healing. Hallelujah!

135

What Comes to Mind

You kept my eyes from closing;
I was too troubled to speak.
I thought about the former days, the years of long ago;
I remembered my songs in the night.

PSALM 77:4-6

have been staring at the ceiling for hours. I feel the urgency to talk to you. But there is silence, so I stare and wonder and ponder. Then I begin to remember all the times you have been there for me. All the times I watched with amazement as you shaped a trial into a treasure, a struggle into a strength.

You speak to me now through these remembrances. I am not alone. I never have been. And this is what you remind me of over and over through your acts of faithfulness.

136

Tell Me

*Make up your mind not to worry beforehand
how you will defend yourselves. For I will
give you words and wisdom that none of your
adversaries will be able to resist or contradict.*

LUKE 21:14-15

Just when I think I have everything all figured out,
somebody challenges me or tears down my securities. The right words never seem to rise to my mind and to my mouth to dispute what they are saying, so here I am wanting to figure it all out beforehand. I don't want any surprises tomorrow. Help me, Lord.

Peace comes over me as I ask for your help. You are not going to provide me with advance comments to memorize before confrontation. Instead, you tell me to reflect on your faithfulness and goodness, and the words and strength I need will be there.

Life Management

*The hardworking farmer should be the first to receive
a share of the crops. Reflect on what I am saying,
for the Lord will give you insight into all this.*

2 TIMOTHY 2:6-7

have an entire shelf of life-management books. They
offer some wisdom and some advice, but they fall
short of insight that relates to my life specifically. How
grateful I am that I have your truth and your Word to
reflect on.

You don't generalize or tell me the top five ways I
will improve my existence or my bank account. You
tell me there is just one way to manage my life—to
give it over to you. My hard work will possibly reap
character development, financial support, and positive
results. But I never have to earn your grace—this is the
key to success.

138

Everything in Its Place

When I consider your heavens, the work of your fingers,
the moon and the stars, which you have set in place,
what is mankind that you are mindful of them,
human beings that you care for them?

PSALM 8:3-4

A night sky tells me much of your nature. When I reflect on the miracle of starlight, the pull of the moon, the orbit of the earth, and the mysteries of space, I feel small and insignificant. But then I consider how much order and brilliance it took to construct this night sky, and I know what I need to know to have hope: The same care and attention went into the creation of me.

When you placed my heart just so and aligned my purpose with your will, there was nothing left to chance. I don't need to question whether you think of me because your fingers shaped me. This life you have set in motion is here for a reason.

139

Longing for Company

*And now, Israel, what does the LORD your God ask of you but
to fear the LORD your God, to walk in obedience to him, to
love him, to serve the LORD your God with all your heart
and with all your soul, and to observe the LORD's commands
and decrees that I am giving you today for your own good?*

DEUTERONOMY 10:12-13

When was the last time I spoke to you from my
heart? Some days bring trials, others bring joy.
Today brings a mixture of both. I'm thankful to now
enter into your presence because I was longing for your
company without even knowing it.

Is my day going as you planned? Am I missing
something wonderful, important, divine? Help me
embrace today's complexities, questions, and ordinary demands. Merely sitting here in your presence is
changing my outlook for the rest of today. I needed a
reminder that you are walking beside me. My pace has
been so fast, sometimes even reckless, that I forgot how
steady a moment can be when I give my heart, soul,
and attention to my Creator.

140

Waiting to Talk

You will call and I will answer you;
you will long for the creature your hands have made.

JOB 14:15

have allowed days and days to go by without talking to you, Lord. In fact, a whole season of life seems to have blurred by while I tapped my fingers and waited for change, peace, better things. Why, in a time of drought, do I forget to pray for rain? I have failed to keep up my end of the dialogue in the past, and you have been faithful. I suppose it is because you have not left. You wait. You move in and through my life and wait for me to respond.

So I call to you today, Lord. On my knees I bow before you and pray for you to hear me. Before your presence covers me, I taste the dryness of desperate longing. I understand what it means to wait for a response from someone I love.

|4|

Savoring

A longing fulfilled is sweet to the soul,
but fools detest turning from evil.

PROVERBS 13:19

Be careful what you wish for." Oh, the wise sayings of man! But it is true. The rush of claiming an object of longing pushes aside any thought of consequences. I know I set my sights on desires that are not of you. But the pursuit can be sweet nonetheless. Lord, help me see how these worldly prizes are empty.

Turn my eyes and spirit from the road leading to ruin. Set my path in the right direction. Give my heart a passion for your knowledge, grace, and love. When earthly longings enter my field of vision, let me see them for what they are: distractions. Let nothing keep me from absolute fulfillment in you. Let me savor your sweetness.

142

A Better Country

They were longing for a better country—a heavenly one. Therefore God is not ashamed to be called their God, for he has prepared a city for them.

HEBREWS 11:16

My days have been crazy, God. I want to abandon my life right now and give it to you with instructions to fix it all. Some choices of mine have complicated matters. My inability to say no to requests for time and energy is now binding my feet and hands. I cannot move toward any greater purpose until I am freed.

So give me clarity today, Lord. Tell me which way to go, how to say no, when to say yes. As your child I long for the days of heaven's glory and ease. Oh, how I hope there is ease. Meanwhile, I hold on to you and ask you to lead me through this life until I can come home.

143

Resting in Promises

Moses also said, "You will know that it was the LORD
when he gives you meat to eat in the evening and
all the bread you want in the morning, because
he has heard your grumbling against him."

EXODUS 16:8

Why don't I learn to be quiet? I have been grumbling about my circumstances for so long that even I cannot bear to listen. When others face bigger troubles, I am quick to suggest my turmoil is of great weight and concern. I tell my story of woe over and over.

Lord, you silence my restless spirit and my rampant complaints. I look around me at the provision so obviously from your hand, and I am unable to find the silly words that flowed easily before. Peace overcomes me, and I rest in the promises that shine forth even when I do not deserve them.

| 44

Which Way to Go?

Sow your seed in the morning,
and at evening let not your hands be idle,
for you do not know which will succeed,
whether this or that, or whether
both will do equally well.

ECCLESIASTES 11:6

Should I go this way...or that way? Tomorrow I will face a fork in the road, and both directions will look so very tempting. This question keeps me awake because I have allowed myself to become restless. Pacing in the living room does not still my mind or my heart. Give me an answer, Lord. Please.

You remind me to fall to my knees in prayer and supplication and thanksgiving. My hands reach for your Word, and this purpose calms them. Now I am feeding my spirit with certainty over uncertainty. And this night I give my doubts over to your control.

Chasing Fears

*Do not worry, saying, "What shall we eat?" or "What
shall we drink?" or "What shall we wear?" For
the pagans run after all these things, and your
heavenly Father knows that you need them. But
seek first his kingdom and his righteousness, and
all these things will be given to you as well.*

MATTHEW 6:31-33

It is futile to chase after fear, for fear leaves in its wake a
very new path of problems. The people I want to guarantee me security are only people. Their promises do
not mean anything to me and my eternal future.

I will not waste my time, my day, my night in this
pursuit of unnecessary concerns. I need not glance
around nervously, anticipating the next problem. You
assure me that I need only to look to you and your
kingdom. Here true needs are recognized, and they are
filled, satisfied by your grace.

146

This, I'm Not Good At

Be still before the LORD
and wait patiently for him.

PSALM 37:7

have loved you for so long, Lord. I have become a person who prays earnestly and with vulnerability. My speech is becoming filled with words of encouragement and hope. I seek your Word with deep hunger because there were too many years when I sought nourishment from empty sources.

But God…I am not good at being still before you. There is a part of me that wants to rush the process, wants to leap forward to the promise fulfilled, and wants to take the reins of my life from your hands. Help me grow in patience. Keep me from the desire to disrupt your plan for my life. I am ready for this lesson.

147

Heart and Soul

Now devote your heart and soul to
seeking the LORD your God.

1 CHRONICLES 22:19

Lord, do I pursue you as I should? I have had hobbies take over my life. Do I give you the same attention? I spend countless hours perusing bookstores and immersing myself in the riches of the written word. When was the last time I gave my spiritual quest the same amount of energy? It's been a while.

I realize I have become lax in my pursuit of you, Lord. You and my faith should occupy my mind more than a part-time interest. Infuse my soul with a desire to pursue you wholly. Completely. I want to know everything about you. I hunger for your Word. I devote my heart and soul to seeking you and your will for my life.

148

Name Above All Names

Those who know your name trust in you,
for you, LORD, have never forsaken those who seek you.

PSALM 9:10

I know your name so well, Lord. I whisper it in times of sorrow. I hold it close when entering a place of fear. I shout its praise during times of celebration. You have carved it on my heart so that I will never forget the Creator of my soul. I do not go anywhere without being covered by your name, for it is powerful.

When I experience doubt, Lord, remind me that "he will be called Wonderful Counselor, Mighty God, Everlasting Father, Prince of Peace." You are all these things to me, Lord. Let me never forget to call on you, the One who does not forsake me but leads me to higher places.

149

Thoughts of God

In his pride the wicked man does not seek him;
in all his thoughts there is no room for God.

PSALM 10:4

Lord, reveal to me the areas where I am prideful. What causes me to stumble while trying to do your will? Obstacles grow in size and threaten to become permanent in my life. They hinder my view of your face. Even though it will be painful and humbling, please remove these barriers to a holy life.

Heal me from blindness caused by self-focus. When my eyes turn only toward my own life, I lose sight of the future you have for me. My worries weigh me down and immobilize me when I should be seeking your freedom. Lord, please take away my selfish thoughts. They crowd out your voice, the voice that gives me purpose.

150

Justice for All

Many seek an audience with a ruler,
but it is from the Lord that one gets justice.

PROVERBS 29:26

I want to be heard, Lord. I always want to tell my side of a situation so an authority can vindicate me. But it is you, Lord, who should receive my call for justice. You are the judge of my soul and my life—why should I seek out any other rulers? In the same way, help me to resist determining the fate of another. It is not my right to stand in your place.

Lord, guide me in your ways when there is conflict. Fill me with wisdom, honesty, and courage, and let me rely on their strength if I am accused. Keep me blameless so no harm is brought to your name. Guard my heart from resentment if I am not treated fairly. May I live out forgiveness and faith, anticipating the justice of love I will receive when in your presence.

|5|

The Promise of Waiting

*In the morning, LORD, you hear my voice;
in the morning I lay my requests before you
and wait expectantly.*

PSALM 5:3

I never viewed waiting as a pleasant experience, Lord. I expected what I wanted, when I wanted it. But you have shown me your care during the waiting hours. I have heard your voice in the whisper of morning and the tiptoe silence of night.

Today I place my need for direction and instruction at your feet and I wait. You provide all that I need during this time of anticipation. Now I understand that the promise of waiting is hope.

152

What Is the Right Choice?

I sought the LORD, and he answered me;
he delivered me from all my fears.

PSALM 34:4

God, I am at a crossroads. I don't know which way to go. Friends have advice; I have my inclinations. But I am fearful. My feet don't want to budge. I have made mistakes and miscalculations before. My spirit has been crushed by broken expectations.

Lord, I am coming to you today completely in awe of your mercy and your faithfulness. I seek your wisdom. I want your confidence as I step forward. Please deliver me from doubt so I can discover the fullness of life.

153

Prevailing Plans

Many are the plans in a person's heart,
but it is the LORD's purpose that prevails.

PROVERBS 19:21

Beneath my actions and my dreams, my hopes and my efforts is a current of purpose set in motion by your hand. As much as I seek your heart, I am not always certain if my desires are of your great plan for me. But day by day I give to you my devotion and my best intentions.

Please mold my human efforts into your divine plan. Create in me a sensitivity to your leading so that I serve a purpose bigger than my own. Take my tightly held heart. Reshape it. Let it expand to fit that place you have made for me in this world. Help me to not settle for a life of busyness that does not make room for what I should be doing. You have something far greater for me to grow into: your purpose for my life.

154

My Purpose in Your Church

*If you have any encouragement from being
united with Christ, if any comfort from his
love, if any common sharing in the Spirit, if any
tenderness and compassion, then make my joy
complete by being like-minded, having the same
love, being one in spirit and of one mind.*

PHILIPPIANS 2:1-2

Lord, help me to be like-minded with my community of fellowship. Guide me to compassion when in the presence of others' pain. Let me tend to people with the love you give. Empower me with a spirit of willingness to work with your children.

I see a display of your character wherever people are gathered, Lord. Our differences balance into wholeness through your grace. It can be so difficult to look past the human idiosyncrasies. They distract us. They give us excuses to place people in categories or push them away. Let me see a person as a whole being. A physical, intellectual, and spiritual child of God. I pray that my actions will always help and not hinder the body of Christ's progression toward your purpose.

How God Works

We know that in all things God works for the good of those who love him, who have been called according to his purpose.

ROMANS 8:28

Lately, not many things seem to be working together for good, Lord. I am not complaining, just stating it like it is. But of course, I don't see as far down the road as you do…and perhaps a few of these situations just didn't work out in my favor. As I revisit the circumstances, maybe these moments were not about my personal success, but someone else's. Did I handle it well, Lord?

I pray for a sense of your grand vision. Help me take every disappointing event, answer, and outcome and look at it from your perspective. I may not see evidence of your plan, so let me rest in my knowledge of your love. Grant my heart peace when I am uncertain of the road I travel, Lord. I will keep moving, one foot in front of the other, because I have been called to good things.

156

Your Power

*It does not, therefore, depend on man's desire or
effort, but on God's mercy. For Scripture says to
Pharaoh: "I raised you up for this very purpose,
that I might display my power in you and that my
name might be proclaimed in all the earth."*

ROMANS 9:16-17

Some people don't see the full me. They know I am a person of faith. They see the job I have and the friends I have made. But, Lord, when I take risks, when I make leaps of faith, may they truly see you and your power.

Only you can lift me up to a place of influence or strength. May I tell everyone what you have done in my life. May your great purposes be seen in the smallest actions of my day.

My Work, My Purpose

The one who plants and the one who waters have one purpose, and they will each be rewarded according to their own labor. For we are co-workers in God's service; you are God's field, God's building.

1 CORINTHIANS 3:8-9

God, the labor you have given me is important, vital, and significant to the building of your purpose. Why do I forget this? I steal hope from your plan by regretting or coveting the labor of others. Show me the work that is mine. Renew my spirit of faithfulness so I may once again taste the satisfaction of committing to the task before me with conviction and joy.

Lord, I want to praise you with all that I do. May I find pleasure and a measure for contentment and ministry in the work you give me each day.

Encouraged

My goal is that they may be encouraged in heart and united in love, so that they may have the full riches of complete understanding, in order that they may know the mystery of God, namely, Christ, in whom are hidden all the treasures of wisdom and knowledge.

COLOSSIANS 2:2-3

When I am discouraged, I take heart in the love you show me. I have witnessed your mercy in the kindness of others, your peace in the blessing of friendship, your wisdom in the Word. These glimpses of who you are add dimension and clarity to my understanding of what gives this life meaning. You are my purpose. And your love lifts me out of my moments of despair and fills my heart with treasures of eternity.

Here to There

*Let perseverance finish its work so that you may
be mature and complete, not lacking anything.*

JAMES 1:4

I think about the large gap between where I am and where I want to be. I don't mean financially or professionally, but in the ways of faith. I want to know you more intimately and take your precepts to heart.

Each day is a new opportunity to become more Christlike. Hold me accountable, Lord. Keep me in the company of those who will encourage and challenge me. Between here to there is a leap of faith, but I'm ready to feel my feet leave the ground as my heart and spirit compel me toward the life of belief and beauty you have for me.

160

Looking for the Line

*Now finish the work, so that your eager
willingness to do it may be matched by your
completion of it, according to your means.*

2 CORINTHIANS 8:11

My home is overrun with half-finished projects and partially read books. I started and stopped four exercise programs last year alone. So what makes me think I can continue in my faith and complete the task of growing in you? I don't know what the finish line will look like, but I am watching for it. I am being perfected in your grace, and I am becoming more excited about fulfilling your purpose for my life.

The finish line is up ahead, and I know you are shaping the twists and turns of my race to get me there.

161

Reaching for the Baton

*I have fought the good fight, I have finished
the race, I have kept the faith.*

2 TIMOTHY 4:7

My pursuit of complete faith has become a relay. Lord, you have given me so many prayer warriors, encouragers, and godly examples to follow. Each one of them provides me with a baton of wisdom and the belief that I can go further. Now I eagerly watch for the next lesson that will mold my view of what it means to be your child.

Past discouragements are completely out of view and out of mind. I have kept the faith, and you, Lord, have kept me fighting the good fight.

162

No More Settling

*I consider my life worth nothing to me; my
only aim is to finish the race and complete the
task the Lord Jesus has given me—the task of
testifying to the good news of God's grace.*

ACTS 20:24

All I wanted to accomplish today was to survive. My
plate was so full, and I felt overwhelmed. How
often do I settle for such a limited view of my day's purpose? "I just want to get by" turns into "Where did last
month go?" I'm caught in a faithless rut.

Lord, give me a deeper vision for tomorrow. The
completion of one day is the continuation of a bigger
plan. I pray my life will be a testimony to your grace.
Turn my limited goals into grander, eternal passions.

163

Embracing the Unknown

Show me your ways, LORD,
teach me your paths.

PSALM 25:4

Father in heaven, you see all that takes place in my life. Knowing this gives me peace as I face transition. I exchange my uncertainty for your promise of security. Open my eyes to the wonders of every turn, tangent, and seeming detour I encounter. I don't want to miss a miracle by starting a new journey diminished by regret, pride, or misplaced longing. I want to long for you. For the path you carve out for me.

Remove the blinders from my physical and spiritual eyes, Lord. I want to see the beauty of the landscape you have built around me. And I want to believe in the opportunity that rests on the horizon. As I face a new direction, this time my heart flutters with excitement and not with worry. I am eager to see what you have in store for me. I accept your provision, Lord.

164

Doing Good

As we have opportunity, let us do good to all people,
especially to those who belong to the family of believers.

GALATIANS 6:10

Where can I do the most good, Lord? Direct me. Guide me to the people you want me to serve. I used to give only to random causes and organizations. My offering at church became my "I gave at the office" excuse when other needs arose. Then, Lord, you allowed me to personally experience small kindnesses. I came to understand how the little matters mean the most. Create a clean motive in my heart, God. May I do good purely to honor you, and not my own reputation. Help me reach out and establish real relationships.

Even if my encounter with a person is for one day, one hour, one smile, this is my opportunity to serve you. I will wait, watch, and act on these opportunities.

165

Choosing Peace

*If it is possible, as far as it depends on
you, live at peace with everyone.*

ROMANS 12:18

Lord, I long for your peace in my soul. I wish to draw it in and release it to others. Where I have a chance to act out your peace, please let me be strong and brave. Conflict is easier sometimes. It allows me to build barriers between me and another, or between me and the right way. But there is little comfort when I stand alone, indignant on one side of the wall.

May I meditate on your Word so that it rises to my mind in place of angry and defensive language. Peace flows from you and into my life. I know its power to change behavior and remove blindness. Grant me the opportunity to share this gift.

166

Opportunity of a Lifetime

He replied, "You are talking like a foolish woman. Shall we accept good from God, and not trouble?"

JOB 2:10

When my timeline, career, family life, and spiritual walk are going as planned, I accept your ways, Lord. I rest in how rewarding my faith can be. But when I face hardship, I assume you have left me or have caused me pain. I know this is not truth. You do not give us more than we are able to bear. God, help me sense your active presence. Teach me your mercy so that I never question it again. Give my heart a measure of promise to keep me going.

Plant in me a trust that will take firm root. Help me recall the previous times when difficulties turned into lessons, strength, and even blessing. May I see every obstacle as an opportunity to accept all that you have for me.

What's Next?

The LORD will vindicate me;
your love, LORD, endures forever—
do not abandon the works of your hands.

PSALM 138:8

Don't stop now, Lord. I am finally catching your vision for my life. It has taken me a while, and I've had to walk through a lot of mistakes, but I am here and ready to receive your purpose. What would you have me do next? Your patience over the years has shown me that you will not abandon the work you have begun. Lead me to the next step.

When I listen to others or even to my own negative thoughts, I am tempted to quit trying. Your love inspires me to keep going. And each time I move forward, my step is more steady. I am certain you will follow through. And I will follow your example. So, what's next?

168

Different Gifts of the Same Spirit

There are different kinds of gifts, but the same Spirit. There are different kinds of service, but the same Lord. There are different kinds of working, but the same God works all of them in all men.

1 CORINTHIANS 12:4-6

Lord, I stand in awe of your love, which is so great…so great that you have made each one of your children unique, special, and miraculous. Our differences are not discerned just in physical characteristics or the language we speak, they are found in a kaleidoscope of gifts—all from the same Spirit.

Often my weakness is another's point of strength—my certainty, another's roadblock of doubt. You have created us to work together. Help me to acknowledge the gifts of others. I want to encourage the people I interact with to do and be their best…your best. Guide my words, Lord, so that I express kindness and inspiration to my family, colleagues, and friends.

All I Have

*As Jesus looked up, he saw the rich putting their gifts into
the temple treasury. He also saw a poor widow put in two
very small copper coins. "Truly I tell you," he said, "this
poor widow has put in more than all the others. All
these people gave their gifts out of their wealth; but
she out of her poverty put in all she had to live on."*

LUKE 21:1-4

Forgive me for how tightly I hold on to the blessings
in my life. I am too cautious in my giving. I even
question how the one I give to will use my offering, as
if that has anything to do with what giving is about.
Along the way I have forgotten that giving is an act of
sacrifice. It is an offering without strings, an expression of your grace.

I don't want to hold back, Lord. I want to freely
stretch out my hand to provide help, a blessing, a commitment to another. Prevent my heart from monitor-
ing, counting, adjusting what I give. May I never keep
track of such things. With your gift of salvation as my
only measure, I pray to give all I have in every moment.

These Are My Gifts

On coming to the house, they saw the child with his mother Mary, and they bowed down and worshiped him. Then they opened their treasures and presented him with gifts of gold, incense and myrrh.

MATTHEW 2:11

I open the treasure of my heart and look for gifts to give you, my King. My offerings reflect the ways I worship you each day. Love for my family. Kindness to others. Help in the face of need. Faith in the future. Trust through doubt. Lord, please accept these as responses of my deep affection for you.

I bow down to you, Lord. Your grace transforms my simple presents into precious metals and expensive oils and perfume. Help me to watch for opportunities to serve you by giving the gift of myself to others. And let me recognize when I am receiving treasured pieces of another's heart.

|71|

Following Directions

Walk in obedience to all that the LORD your God has commanded you, so that you may live and prosper and prolong your days in the land that you will possess.

DEUTERONOMY 5:33

Lord, from your vantage point, the charting of my daily course must look like a very unorganized spider's web. Here. There. Back again. How many days do I spend running in circles to keep up with the life I've created? Lead me to the life you planned for me. Unravel those strands of confusion and weave together a course that is of your design.

This new vision for my life involves asking you for directions. Remind me of the beautiful pattern my steps can create when I seek your help—when I feel lost and when I feel in control. Lord, give me the insight to follow your commands. Guide me toward my true life.

172

Guiding Force of Nature

He loads the clouds with moisture;
he scatters his lightning through them.
At his direction they swirl around over the face of the
whole earth to do whatever he commands them.

JOB 37:11-12

Lord, your hand choreographs the dance of nature. You speak forth the rhythm of the ocean waves. Your word commands the clouds to rain on the thirsty land. The precise action and inaction of every element is under your instruction. Why do I challenge the force of your will in my life? I need only to witness the power of a stormy day or watch the sun dissolve into the horizon to know that you rule over all living things.

The beauty of creation can be mirrored in my own life. I must first give myself over to the dance that you choreograph. May I leap with full joy. Let my sweeping bow follow your grace. And as I stretch heavenward with open arms, may I be ready to receive the loving guidance you pour over my life.

173

Moving into God's Love

May the Lord direct your hearts into God's love and Christ's perseverance.

2 THESSALONIANS 3:5

Lord, I confess I have been playing tug-of-war with you. As you start to pull my heartstrings in one direction, I stubbornly resist. Goals and aims other than your best dazzle me with cheap imitations of love. I avert my gaze for just a moment and lose sight of your plan. Instill in me a steadfast heart. Let me be single-minded in my faith and trust.

Allow me to persevere in the direction you want me to go. Let me not be tempted by false gods or deceptive voices, which lead me astray. I should never play games with my heart. After all, it belongs to you. Take it now, Lord. I don't want to halt the beat of your love in my life.

174

A Parent's Instruction

*My son, keep your father's command
and do not forsake your mother's teaching...
When you walk, they will guide you.*

PROVERBS 6:20,22

Don't touch the stove." "Look both ways." "Don't hit your sister." "Say you're sorry." Lord, the earliest instructions from my parents became lessons for my spiritual growth. The concept of cause and effect seeped past my resistance. Eventually I saw how parental guidance was about protection and concern.

Your commands reflect this truth from my childhood. I know that you guard my steps because you love me. I look to you before I proceed with a plan. I await your approving nod before I make commitments and promises. Your Word lights my way even when I have run so far ahead that your voice seems faint. Lord, may I always hear and heed your directions. Guide me toward a righteous life.

Stepping Toward Fulfillment

"Love your neighbor as yourself." Love does no harm to
a neighbor. Therefore love is the fulfillment of the law.

ROMANS 13:9-10

Lord, you have shown me that the key to life, to connection, to relationship, and to purpose is to love. May I have the strength to draw inspiration and motivation from your love so that I may share it with others—that I might experience deep fulfillment.

I am not sure I know how to define "fulfillment." But sometimes I get a glimpse of what it looks like in the smile of others; I get a feel for it when I sense your hand on my life. Teach me to truly understand what it means to be filled by love's grace. And when I have understanding, teach me to move deeper into the offerings of a fulfilled life.

176

My First Glance

Satisfy us in the morning with your unfailing love,
that we may sing for joy and be glad all our days.

PSALM 90:14

There are days when I hate the sound of the alarm and don't feel ready to see the light of another morning. This is a sure sign that I have been walking through my human experience in my own power and purpose. That is not satisfying. That is not compelling.

Today I will let myself sit back and enjoy the warmth of a new day's greeting. Lord, you are so faithful. You give me everything I need for each moment, each day, each stretch of my path. I will use my voice to sing for joy and shout my praises to you for the gift of possibility you provide with each new dawn. May I be glad all of my days, and may I bring you gladness and glory with all of my life. Thank you.

177

Taking Vows

*Then will I ever sing praise to your name
and fulfill my vows day after day.*

PSALM 61:8

God, the day I made my commitment to follow you and seek your heart, I entered into a covenant that would change my life forever. Today, with disappointment in myself, I look back over times when I didn't fulfill my part of the covenant. I let go when I should have held on tighter. Forgive me for the moments when I became casual about nurturing my relationship with you.

The act of taking a vow ushers us into a living, breathing, changing relationship. Because of your unconditional love, this is a relationship of grace. I praise you today, Lord, because your covenant remains unbroken. And I sing your praises because I long to fulfill my vows of faith in your presence.

178

First Time

God said, "Let there be light," and there was light.
God saw that the light was good, and he separated
the light from the darkness. God called the light "day,"
and the darkness he called "night." And there was
evening, and there was morning—the first day.

GENESIS 1:3-5

I wonder what the first night looked like. How did you arrange the sky? Did you watch the sun go down and imagine how your future creation would love the sight of such beauty?

Lord, I thank you for that time when day becomes night. I allow that time to come and go so often without speaking words of gratitude. Tonight I will notice how you transform the view from my window and be reminded of the hope I have in how you are transforming me.

Goodness of a Bad Day

Though outwardly we are wasting away, yet
inwardly we are being renewed day by day. For our
light and momentary troubles are achieving for
us an eternal glory that far outweighs them all.

2 Corinthians 4:16-17

I've had one of those days recently. The kind that unfolded with a series of errors, miscommunications, and missteps. It'd be nice to forget about the disaster of a day, but I know that while I am experiencing those bumps in the road, there are more eternal activities in play.

When I stumble, there is still victory. You transform my very human errors into pearls of internal value. I have learned humility, perseverance, faith, and patience. Not bad for a day's work.

180

New Thoughts

Repent, then, and turn to God, so that
your sins may be wiped out, that times of
refreshing may come from the Lord.

ACTS 3:19

like stability. I like it so much that I unintentionally create each day to look the same as the last. I fall into ruts that do nothing to serve you or this life you have given to me. I pray for the wisdom to infuse my life with renewal and possibility. I don't want my days to be staid and fruitless. Such apathy is more likely to lead to sin than spiritual growth.

When I am burdened with repetition and routine, remind me how much each day is worth. When I maneuver on autopilot, awaken me to think differently, feel differently, and to honor the different moments that add up to my lifetime. Refresh me, dear God.

Your Power

*I will turn the darkness into light before them
and make the rough places smooth.*

ISAIAH 42:16

God, you orchestrate the universe without need of my help. You turn darkness into light just like that—in your power. There is nothing you can't do on your own; yet, you choose to use and include your flawed and sometimes fearful children. I'm so humbled that you work through me, and that you see value in who I am and in this life I'm living.

I rest in the knowledge that you shape my heart and my journey. You transform the rough places I stumble over into smooth paths with your mercy. Best of all, you allow me to enter the world filled with your power to love, serve, forgive, and be a light in the dark.

182

My Backbone

May integrity and uprightness protect me,
because my hope, LORD, is in you.

PSALM 25:21

In my faith, I have discovered the secret to standing tall in the world. When I threw away my desire to put myself first, I came upon your will and your purpose for my life. This gift has given me the security to be at peace with the way life unfolds. My hope is not in guaranteed profit, certain success, or the perfect relationship. My hope is in you, and when I face choices and changes, I measure my response according to the integrity your love gives to me.

To be secure in a loving and knowing God, I knew I would have to let go of my unreal expectations so that I could make room for your unbelievable promises. It was the best decision I ever made. Thank you for giving me what I needed to stand tall and to walk with hope.

A Worthy Friend

*Teach the older women to be reverent in the way
they live, not to be slanderers or addicted to much
wine, but to teach what is good. Then they can
urge the younger women to love their husbands
and children, to be self-controlled and pure, to be
busy at home, to be kind, and to be subject to their
husbands, so that no one will malign the word of God.*

TITUS 2:3-5

Thank you for the relationships I have with other women. Some of them previously walked through the experiences I'm currently having. Their shared wisdom encourages me to keep going, to take a new look at my situation, to be thankful for the process of living. My kinship with younger women is also fulfilling. I understand the role I can play as mentor, friend, confidante, and prayer partner. Lord, in all my relationships with women, help me to be a good friend who reflects grace, not judgment; who offers support, not competition; who gives hope, not anxiety.

184

It Is Personal

For your Maker is your husband—
the LORD Almighty is his name—
the Holy One of Israel is your Redeemer;
he is called the God of all the earth.

ISAIAH 54:5

You are the love of my life. You are the Lord of my life. You care for and nourish my soul because you created it with all of its needs, intricacies, and mysteries. The times when other people let me down, or when I let myself down, you lifted me up on wings of your faithfulness.

Some days I do not know myself well. I question my actions and my direction. My comfort is in you. You speak to the depths of my being and remind me that I am yours, and that is all that matters. You are called the God of all the earth, and you have a personal relationship with me. Thank you, Lord.

185

Serving One Another

Each one of you also must love his wife as he loves himself, and the wife must respect her husband.

EPHESIANS 5:33

Marriage is a precious gift. God, please watch over my marriage relationship. Help me respect the dreams and choices of my husband. Guide him to love and cherish me as we work together toward our future. I pray that we will always rely on you for guidance and direction.

Let us follow your example of unconditional love as we care for one another. God, reveal to us the ways we can serve one another as we also serve you.

186

Love One Another

Dear friends, let us love one another,
for love comes from God.

1 JOHN 4:7

My love comes with limits. I didn't learn that from you, Lord, so why does my heart restrict its capacity to love other people? When I am afraid of commitment, please give me peace to move forward. If I feel I do not have enough love to extend to another person, please urge me to trust your command to love one another.

Love comes directly from you. Let me receive it with grace and give it with peace.

Honest

Each of you must put off falsehood and speak truthfully
to your neighbor, for we are all members of one body.
EPHESIANS 4:25

'm not always good at being sociable. I want to be involved in the lives of other people, but, God, sometimes it is difficult to be myself around others. Making new friends is not easy, even when they are people of faith. I find that my old insecurities rise up and take over my personality when I step into a room of strangers.

Lord, give me the confidence and courage I need to speak from the heart with others and show them the real me. You created me, and I should take comfort in this life I lead and the person I have grown to be. As I speak to others, give me a heart for their concerns, needs, and insecurities so we can all be open with one another.

188

Pure and Simple

*"Martha, Martha," the Lord answered, "you are worried
and upset about many things, but few things are
needed, or indeed only one. Mary has chosen what
is better, and it will not be taken away from her."*

LUKE 10:41-42

I sure do make life complicated, don't I? You don't
need to answer that, Lord. I hear my own thoughts
and watch my actions with dismay. I am quick to
blame others when things go wrong. My truth is based
on me and not on you. I get so caught up in the acts of
fretting and fussing that I lose sight of that one thing I
need—time with you.

Lord, I want a pure and simple relationship with
you. I want to put aside the many distractions and sit at
your feet, ready and willing to know you better.

Something Good

I pray that your partnership with us in the faith
may be effective in deepening your understanding
of every good thing we share for the sake of Christ.

PHILEMON 6

Because of my faith in you, I have something worth sharing. Help me pass along the perfect promises of faith to others even though I am fallible and imperfect. I may not always think of the right words, but I have faith in your Word. I might stumble or falter, but then your power of grace will be noticed.

When I trust you and express the goodness of Christ to people in my life, I become more in tune with your love for them. My heart opens up to include people and to accept them—just as your heart does every day.

190

A Friend's Prayer

*My intercessor is my friend
as my eyes pour out tears to God;
on behalf of a man he pleads with God
as one pleads for a friend.*

JOB 16:20-21

My friend, who knows the Holy Spirit, prays for me. I am greatly comforted by this. I can be tumbling headlong into a hectic day of work, and all of a sudden realize I have been bathed in prayer. I receive peace from the efforts of another.

My words to you come from my heart and are meaningful through the Spirit's interpretation. Yet, I find a deeper comfort knowing that a friend lifts up words to your ears. She calls upon the Holy Spirit to hear her pleas on my behalf. I have a friend who knows Jesus, and we both have a friend in you. Thank you, Lord.

|91|

Friends in High Places

I am a friend to all who fear you,
to all who follow your precepts.

PSALM 119:63

There was a time when I followed the steps of those who did not care about your existence. I emulated their mannerisms, which reflected worldly poise. I am thankful I woke up from this false dream. When I noticed you on the perimeter of life, I knew right away that I had set my sights too low for myself. There was something greater…no, Someone greater to follow.

I thank you for bringing godly people into my life. My path is not always straight. I wander. I take long detours that should be day trips. My friends who know you and fear you with their every breath give me directions back to your way. They stay true to your precepts; you stay true to me.

192

Misplaced Friendship

Anyone who chooses to be a friend of the
world becomes an enemy of God.

JAMES 4:4

Forgive me, Lord, for the times when I choose the world over you. With all you have done for me, I cannot believe I am still tempted by the world. Yet I am. I think it relates to my insecurities. The times when I do not trust you are the times when someone else's success or position in life has influence over my heart. Recently, I have felt a need to be accepted by the world. Forgive me for leaning toward the artificial light of the world when I have the brilliance of your glory in my heart. The trivial needs will pass, and I will be left with truth—your truth. Lead me back to you, Lord. I do not want any part of me to flow against your will… even my longings.

Making a Connection

If either of them falls down,
one can help the other up.
But pity anyone who falls and has
no one to help them up.

ECCLESIASTES 4:10

I have a full life: family, work, church, commitments. But I am missing the connection of a close friend. I have had that in my life, so I understand what is lacking. I turn to you with my concerns and my joys, Lord, just as I should. But I need a friend of the flesh, who experiences the trials of life as I do. You know my heart intimately. Now I want to share it with a special friend.

Please let me be open to whom this friend might be. Perhaps it is someone already in my life. Maybe you are directing a stranger to cross paths with me. I don't want to miss the chance to connect with someone you have chosen for me. I believe friendships lead us to a deeper relationship with you. I cannot wait to meet the special friend you have for me.

194

Seeing Myself

To love him with all your heart, with all your understanding and with all your strength, and to love your neighbor as yourself is more important than all burnt offerings and sacrifices.

MARK 12:33

have gone through many phases in my life. There was a time I tried to do anything and everything. It was my goal to be the busiest person I knew so nobody would think my life was empty. I saw my effort as a form of sacrifice for you. But your gentle voice reminded me to pace myself and to live fully.

Even if I have seasons of loneliness, I know you are present and have not abandoned me. Once you opened my eyes to the needs of others, I noticed my neighbor who faced loss, the friend who needed to talk, and for the first time, I saw me—the person who is far from alone.

195

For the Greater Good

Let us discern for ourselves what is right;
let us learn together what is good.

JOB 34:4

Lead me to those people who are doing good, Lord. Guide my steps and my choices so I am in the presence of people who love you and who work as your hands. I stand with a solid understanding of what is right and what is wrong, but when I stand alone, I feel uninspired. I need the encouragement and community of others to step up my giving and my abundant living.

I want to be counted as one of your faithful children. But I don't always know where to begin. Direct me to the groups or gatherings where you need me. Give me the confidence to join a community that seeks your goodness.

196

Part of the Body

*Just as each of us has one body with many members,
and these members do not all have the same
function, so in Christ we, though many, form one
body, and each member belongs to all the others.*

ROMANS 12:4-5

God, what does the body of Christ look like from afar? Is it a circle? An undistinguishable blob? A river? Are there sections trying to go their own way? I wonder about these things occasionally when I spend time with other believers. I realize how often my own priorities or purposes dictate how I interact with others or how well I follow.

Teach me to be a contributing member of the body of Christ. Allow me to recognize and appreciate my unique abilities and gifts—and then have me use them for your purposes.

197

Complete in Community

*Do nothing out of selfish ambition or vain
conceit. Rather, in humility value others above
yourselves, not looking to your own interests
but each of you to the interests of the others.*

PHILIPPIANS 2:3-4

Unite my heart with others. Remove any barriers I create. When I feel distant from those people who are part of my life, draw me close to someone. And when I initiate comparison, restore my sense of unity in Christ. Allow me to witness the beauty and joy of wholeness and community.

Lord, when I feel the tug on my heart to reach out and connect, let me be faithful in following through with your direction. I see how honoring the gifts you have graciously given is really about making connections with your other children. Your mercy is found in the most mundane situations, and when we least expect it. Help me to watch for your living grace.

Sister Act

Now, you women, hear the word of the LORD;
open your ears to the words of his mouth.
Teach your daughters how to wail;
teach one another a lament.

JEREMIAH 9:20

Do I model your love to other women, Lord? If I could be an example to anyone, I would want to show your truth to women. Part of that truth relates to the ability to tap into one's emotions. Contemporary society requires such poise and control. We forget to teach young women how important it is to feel grief and pain fully. Difficult experiences bring us to your feet. They reveal your mercy.

We grow strong only through our opportunities to rely on you, Lord. My sense of ability comes only from you. I desire to share with other women the security I have found in my Savior. You are not only the epitome of love, but the definition of love. Your love for each of us is meant to be felt deeply.

Ask Father

*Jesus answered her, "If you knew the gift of God and
who it is that asks you for a drink, you would have
asked him and he would have given you living water."*

JOHN 4:10

It took me a long time to drink from the living water.
I felt your presence before but chose to ignore your
offer of salvation. I think of the many bright, accomplished women who do not know you. On the world's
terms, they might seem to be filled with truth and
knowledge, but I know you have much more planned
for their lives.

God, I pray for women who do not yet call you by
name. I pray for the women who see a father figure as
someone who is abusive or critical or unloving. Let
them embrace the Father that I know so dearly and
truly. Show them the true, loving image of the Savior.

200

Keep Talking

*The angel said to the women, "Do not be afraid,
for I know that you are looking for Jesus, who was
crucified. He is not here; he has risen, just as he
said. Come and see the place where he lay. Then
go quickly and tell his disciples: 'He has risen from
the dead and is going ahead of you into Galilee.
There you will see him.' Now I have told you."*

MATTHEW 28:5-7

You give me a wonderful message to share, Lord.
You entrust me with a mighty word to speak to
other people. My personal testimony is not elaborate,
but it contains the miracle of spiritual rebirth. You
revealed your resurrection to women, and your angel
directed them to share the news. I believe you continue
to use women in this way. Your goodness is for every
one of your children. May I follow in the footsteps
of those who loved you when you walked the earth.
And may I continue to believe the wonder I have been
shown: your love.

You Call Me Daughter

Jesus turned and saw her. "Take heart, daughter,"
he said, "your faith has healed you." And
the woman was healed at that moment.

MATTHEW 9:22

Lord, I have shed tears over a particular hurt in my life. Though it is not a recent wound, it reopens when I am most fragile. Like many women, I let the daily stresses distract me from the pain, but eventually the heart and mind return to the source of anxiety. Forgive me, Father, for holding this sorrow within my soul, for thinking I could fix it on my own.

This wound never mended because I have never reached out in desperation to you. I wanted control over my hurts. I was ashamed to come to you. But today my faith leads me to you. I reach for the hem of your robe and believe. And you heal your daughter once and for all.

202

Did I Just Say That?

May these words of my mouth and this meditation
of my heart be pleasing in your sight,
LORD, my Rock and my Redeemer.

PSALM 19:14

Did that bit of gossip just come from me? Did I just vent and leave my coworker frustrated? Was it my voice that commented negatively on someone's best efforts? Grant me wisdom and the ability to self-censor, Lord. How often I waste precious time trying to fix something that I ruined by speaking with reckless words. Let the messages that come from me be ones that build up, inspire, and reflect my Redeemer's heart.

May I continue to seek the peace of my faith so that I will not speak unthinkingly from a restless heart, but will speak only from an unwavering desire to please you.

Words for You

My lips will shout for joy
when I sing praise to you—
I whom you have redeemed.

Psalm 71:23

As words of encouragement leave my lips, I realize that whether I am talking to myself, a friend, a child, or a coworker, I am also speaking to you, Lord. I have not always taken spiritual responsibility for the words that come from me. I would write them off as appropriate for the circumstance or incited by the situation. But lately, as I consider each word to be spoken for you to hear, I weigh each word. Does it praise my Redeemer? Does it offer someone else a gift in any way? Or is it meant to ease my fear, my insecurity?

Lord, grant me a new vocabulary so that my everyday conversations become praises and shouts for joy.

204

Listen to Me

Hear my cry, O God;
listen to my prayer.

PSALM 61:1

Sometimes I can speak all day and not feel heard. I might as well be invisible or mute. Those days start to take away my sense of meaning and purpose, of connection to the world around me. Today is one of those days. All I ask is to be heard, Lord. Please listen to my prayer and turn your heart and ear to my whispered thoughts.

To be heard is to have validation. Each time I fall to my knees and talk to you, I understand who I am. I know that I have purpose. You hear what I say between the words. Even my silence shapes my identity in you, Lord. Hear my cry. Listen to my prayer.

Faith

Immediately the boy's father exclaimed, "I do believe; help me overcome my unbelief!"

MARK 9:24

Lord, as I make my way through life with a heart that has faith, I find I still must return to you and ask for your help to believe. This does not reflect my belief in your presence or your truth. It reflects how I feel about myself in this world. I move questions from the tip of my mind to the depths of my soul each day to make room for work, conversation, polite interaction, and the status quo. But eventually they surface. And when they do, I pray for answers. I pray for your presence. I pray for faith.

I do believe, Lord. Help me overcome my unbelief.

206

My Mother Taught Me

To answer before listening—
that is folly and shame.

PROVERBS 18:13

During my childhood, I was sent to my room a few times for speaking out of turn. Usually I was trying to prove a point—a really good point, of course. Lord, I am not so different as an adult. I am eager to set the record straight. I don't even recognize this fault until it is too late and the words have been spoken.

Lord, convict me when my desire to clarify or correct is hindering a relationship, a conversation, a chance to listen with my whole heart.

207

What Catches My Attention

[Martha] had a sister called Mary, who sat at the Lord's feet listening to what he said. But Martha was distracted by all the preparations that had to be made.

LUKE 10:39-40

worry about my well-being, about my security and future. There is much to be done in order to provide for tomorrow. Such thoughts consume me. You are here with me, and still my mind races with to-do lists, figures, and concerns. Lord, steer me from the distractions that plague me. I want to be the one who will drop anything and everything—my plans, my expectations, my will—to spend time at your feet.

Following you begins with listening to you. Let me put aside my agenda and sit at your feet all my days.

208

Answer Buffet

As for me, I watch in hope for the LORD,
I wait for God my Savior;
my God will hear me.

MICAH 7:7

The world has many answers. My concerns seem ripe for the world's intervention. But I want my hope to be in you alone. I am trying not to listen to advice that is born of commercial pursuits and overeager self-help gurus. I let such guesses pass me by while I wait upon you and your Word.

Hear me now, Lord. Do not let me wait in vain. My eyes are watching and my ears are listening for the Provider of hope and the final answers to all of life's questions.

Tonight

Surely then you will find delight in the Almighty
and will lift up your face to God.
You will pray to him, and he will hear you,
and you will fulfill your vows.

JOB 22:26-27

The time will come when I will face the night with hope. There will be anticipation as I plan to tell you all about my troubles and my heartaches. Right now I am still overcome with my trials. I know you are here, carrying me through them, but I have been reluctant to listen to what you have to tell me.

Tonight I will lift up my face to you and step into your presence wholly.

210

Still

You have searched me, LORD,
and you know me.
You know when I sit and when I rise;
you perceive my thoughts from afar.

PSALM 139:1-2

You know me inside and out, and you *still* love me. You have searched my depths and counted my tears and eased my worries. Nothing I do goes unnoticed by my God. The mistakes I have brought to your feet have been swept away by the rain of your mercy. My failures, complaints, and rants have been forgotten.

There are no obstacles between me and your acceptance. You have had to clear away all my excuses and barriers. And you still love me.

211

Known

Keep on loving one another as brothers and sisters. Do not forget to show hospitality to strangers, for by so doing some people have shown hospitality to angels without knowing it.

HEBREWS 13:1-2

Normally I'm too shy or intimidated or busy to share in conversation with people I do not know. But when there is something in common that sparks a connection with another person, it leads to a real bond. I don't want to miss out on that because of fear, pride, or anxiety.

It is silly how many times I have not followed my impulse to reach out to someone else because of my fear of rejection. Carry me through this initial doubt. And remind me that even when I don't know the person, the person is known and loved by you.

212

Can You Hear Me?

You, Lord, are forgiving and good,
abounding in love to all who call to you.

PSALM 86:5

Lord, hear my prayers today. I have much to bring to you. My mind and heart are filled with concerns and praises. As soon as I opened my eyes this morning, I was aware I needed to talk to you. I have kept my distance for a while because of feelings of shame. My stubbornness caused me to feel unloved and unwanted.

But you are my Redeemer and my Savior. I need not return to my old patterns of thinking and behavior. I can come to you anytime because you love me, you forgive me, and you accept me. I have so much to tell you.

Letting Go

Do not remember the sins of my youth
and my rebellious ways;
according to your love remember me,
for you, LORD, are good.

PSALM 25:7

How many times have you called me to let go of my concerns and accept my own circumstances? How many times have you whispered "Let go" regarding my past sins, stumblings, and moments of indifference? Each time your grace covers me, I wonder if you've forgotten that I just came to you with the same muddled mess. But now I understand that you saved me from those past foibles long ago. And you accept me just as I am today. I'm the one who forgets that you have forgiven the past transgressions. I'm the one holding onto the same bag of retired, useless errors and not believing I can let go of them once and for all. I want to remember. I want to walk in your grace.

Thank you, Lord, for releasing my rebellious ways and for never letting go of me.

214

What I Call Sacred

One person considers one day more sacred than
another; another considers every day alike.

ROMANS 14:5

The hour when day fades to evening can feel sacred. As my mind and spirit become more present to you and less distracted than during the busyness of daytime, I ease into your presence. I'm attentive and receptive. I want to be able to experience this connection with you even during the chaotic days. Even during meetings and activities. Even when I face conflicts and conundrums. What a gift that would be.

When I surrender my life to your grace and guidance, my eyes are opened to witness what is holy and set apart. The time of day doesn't matter. The circumstances are insignificant. The mood I'm in is irrelevant. Every moment is sacred in the shelter of your care.

215

Shelter Me

Keep me safe, my God,
for in you I take refuge.

PSALM 16:1

Shelter me, Lord. Take me in your embrace and keep me safe from the worries I have about the future. If left on my own, I would not make it through the night without a stream of concerns flooding my mind or a stream of tears making their way down my cheeks. But here in your arms I can relax. I think more clearly from this place of refuge.

I used to be a child who didn't know to come in out of the rain. Now I am your child who knows to come in to your presence and out of the pain. Don't let go of me, Lord.

216

Mine and Yours

*In your unfailing love you will lead
the people you have redeemed.
In your strength you will guide them
to your holy dwelling.*

EXODUS 15:13

This is quite a journey I am on. Each day offers more steps toward your holy dwelling, your resting place. When I stumble, you whisper to me that I am worth leading. You reach for my hand and help me to stand and continue.

My weakness is your strength. My failing is your victory. My worst-case scenario is your moment of shining glory. Lord, you shape all my humanness with your power and grace, and it becomes something new. This is the miraculous journey of redemption.

217

Refuge Within

*Create in me a pure heart, O God,
and renew a steadfast spirit within me.*

PSALM 51:10

seek different ways to create a sense of refuge. I organize aspects of my self and space. I try to breathe right and center my thoughts. I've ordered my days with digital calendars and pretty planners. The stress creeps in just the same. It causes my spirit to churn and my hope to wane.

God, now I understand that my sense of refuge will not be created by altering the external factors or my breathing patterns. You shape my heart and prepare a place where you reside. May your purity stir within me and may your love make its home there.

218

Eyes on You

*If I have put my trust in gold or said to pure
gold, "You are my security," if I have rejoiced over
my great wealth, the fortune my hands had gained,
if I have regarded the sun in its radiance or the
moon moving in splendor, so that my heart was
secretly enticed and my hand offered them a kiss of
homage, then these also would be sins to be judged,
for I would have been unfaithful to God on high.*

JOB 31:24-28

Like a magician telling me to watch the coin beneath
the swirling, twirling cups…my eyes try to follow
the money in my life. Where will the wealth be for me?
How will I provide for my future? I blame my lack of a
solid foundation on the fact that I don't get the help I
need and want.

This is when you stop my crazy thinking. I turn
my eyes back to my only source of security and life—
you. You created the certainty in my past and you are
the brightness of my future. I don't need to look any
further.

219

Rich in Spirit

However, there need be no poor people among you, for in the land the Lord your God is giving you to possess as your inheritance, he will richly bless you, if only you fully obey the LORD your God and are careful to follow all these commands I am giving you today.

DEUTERONOMY 15:4-5

am learning to rest in the riches of my faith. Your children are never poor in spirit, and I am so thankful. My desires for the things of the world lessen as my hope in the matters of eternity increases.

There is a fullness in my heart when I think of the day I came to you, asking for your love. To this day, that love overflows into and through every part of my life. I am grateful for my inheritance. It gives me a richer today and a brighter tomorrow. Show me how to give to others from my inheritance, Lord.

220

One More Hour

Who of you by worrying can add a single hour to your life? Since you cannot do this very little thing, why do you worry about the rest?

LUKE 12:25-26

like to be able to reflect and pray. The down side is that those times of solitude or stillness can lead me to wonder and worry about my life, my choices. It isn't that I'm not happy with my life—I feel blessed in many ways. But when I have the television on for company or I seek out distractions to avoid feeling alone and afraid or to keep worries from flooding my mind, then I am also avoiding your presence and care.

Who am I to think I can change anything by fretting about yesterday or today? Teach me to relax. I don't want to spend one more hour serving the god of worry when the God of life and hope is my Lord.

221

Because

You will be secure, because there is hope;
you will look about you and take your rest in safety.

JOB 11:18

My life has drifted. There have been times when I have felt confused about my faith and my personal path. What are you doing, Lord? What would you have *me* do? I have struggled with the meaning of life. It is a cliché, but it is also the truth.

But you call me to look around. You ask me to take inventory of my life and see the proof of your love and direction. Here I finally find peace. I can make sense of my days because there is hope in all you have done for me.

222

Protection

Then Jacob prayed, "O God of my father Abraham, God of my father Isaac, LORD, you who said to me, 'Go back to your country and your relatives, and I will make you prosper,' I am unworthy of all the kindness and faithfulness you have shown your servant. I had only my staff when I crossed this Jordan, but now I have become two camps. Save me, I pray, from the hand of my brother Esau, for I am afraid he will come and attack me, and also the mothers with their children. But you have said, 'I will surely make you prosper and will make your descendants like the sand of the sea, which cannot be counted.'"

GENESIS 32:9-12

God, you provide a secure way for me to head into today and the future days of my life. When I stumble, you offer your hand and lead me through the situation. I have learned faith through the act of perseverance. And I have discovered hope on the other side. Lead me, Lord. Guard my heart from becoming hardened or untrusting. I turn my fragile spirit over to your care, for you are my Father, my Maker, and my Protector.

223

Healing

Have mercy on me, LORD, for I am faint;
heal me, LORD, for my bones are in agony.
My soul is in deep anguish.
How long, LORD, how long?

PSALM 6:2-3

It is easy to break as a human. As a being made of earth, water, and breath, it is easy to crumble and develop holes. Lord, you made me. You know what it takes to heal the places that are broken, underused, and weak.

I give to you my physical, emotional, and spiritual wounds and ask for your touch, your breath, your mercy to cover them. Heal me, Lord.

224

No Charge

*As you go, proclaim this message: "The kingdom of heaven
has come near." Heal the sick, raise the dead, cleanse those
who have leprosy, drive out demons. Freely you have received;
freely give. Do not get any gold or silver or copper to take
wiht you in your belts—no bag for the journey or extra
shirt or sandals or a staff, for the worker is worth his keep.*

MATTHEW 10:7-10

Doctors, appointments, and expensive medications...
that's what is involved in physical healing these days.
But I look back on the way you healed people in the past
and realize it was done from your power and without
strings. You even sent out your disciples with instruction to not take anything in exchange for healing others.

When I next face the need for physical healing, may
I first come to you with my requests. I will pray for my
doctors and my ability to make wise health decisions.
And after I pay my deductible to humans, I will praise
your name for the "free of charge" healing of the spirit
that takes place each time I place my trust in the power
of your love.

225

Restored

*When Jesus came into Peter's house, he saw Peter's
mother-in-law lying in bed with a fever. He
touched her hand and the fever left her, and
she got up and began to wait on him.*

MATTHEW 8:14-15

You hear my prayers for healing and wholeness,
Lord. I call out to you during a night of pain and
heartache. I believe in your healing touch. When
your peace replaces my brokenness, I pray that I will
be grateful. When my fatigue eases into energy and
strength, I pray that I will in turn wait on you and obey
your commands with renewed commitment.

Lord, you touched me and healed me. I praise you,
and may I never forget who is the Light when I come
out of the darkness.

226

Cover Me

*Keep me safe, LORD, from the hands of the wicked;
protect me from the violent
who devise ways to trip my feet.*

PSALM 140:4

Lord, save me from my fear of the unknown. I read and see enough news about the violence that exists beyond my front door. Do not let this consume me, this possible pain. Give me courage to trust you with the steps I take beyond this threshold. Lord, I believe you will protect me. And if something should happen, I believe you would not abandon me.

I know I cannot avoid living fully just because there is risk of physical harm. Keep me from harm's way. Speak to my heart and give me the presence of mind to listen to your guidance.

Remembering to Ask

Jesus stopped and ordered the man to be brought to him. When he came near, Jesus asked him, "What do you want me to do for you?" "Lord, I want to see," he replied. Jesus said to him, "Receive your sight; your faith has healed you." Immediately he received his sight and followed Jesus, praising God. When all the people saw it, they also praised God.

LUKE 18:40-43

believe I have carried around this hurt for a long time. I might find temporary solutions that ease the discomfort or ways to distract my mind from the pain, but I have not done the most basic thing. I have not told you, my God and Savior, what I need. I have not prayed for healing.

God, my own uncertainties have kept me from falling at your feet and asking you for help. Give me strength to hold on to this kind of faith at all times. I pray that my circumstance will become an opportunity for other people to see your power and to praise your mighty name.

228

Save My Heart

Turn to me and be gracious to me,
for I am lonely and afflicted.

PSALM 25:16

Look at me, God. I am sad…lonely even. It takes so much for my heart to feel alive these days. I am so distant from those things that used to bring me joy. This is not who I want to be. This is not who you want your child to be.

Turn to me, Lord. Heal my brokenness so that I can hold my faith in the warmth of the sun and carry it with me throughout the day. I do not know when I changed so drastically. But I do know that you have not changed. You are the Healer of wounds inside and out. You are the One who sees me and sees my trouble without turning away. Turn to me. Let me feel the sun. Turn to me.

229

Stepping out of the Fog

Restore us, O God;
make your face shine on us,
that we may be saved.

PSALM 80:3

My mind is foggy. I have stepped behind a shroud of stress, distance, and emotional indifference. I view everything through this haze. I want to walk through my life awake and with great passion, Lord. Pull away my self-protective layers so that I know and trust your will.

Restore my mind and my heart, Lord. While I have been surviving through the days, you have wanted me to be transformed. You desire for me to feel the emotional highs and lows that create the landscape of life. I am ready to wake up, Lord. Shine on me.

230

The Fear Factor

Peter got down out of the boat, walked on the water and came toward Jesus. But when he saw the wind, he was afraid and, beginning to sink, cried out, "Lord, save me!"

MATTHEW 14:29-30

Give me courage, Lord. Facing risk is not just a matter of trusting you. It also becomes a matter of defying the power of fear. When Peter walked on the water at your command, he was held up, kept from being hurt by the storm's strength. But as soon as he let the fear and doubt creep back into his spirit, he began to sink.

I do not want to go under the waves of worry that are just waiting to crash down upon me. Lord, carry me to the shore of emotional safety. Protect my mind from anxiousness. I will keep my eyes upon you, and I will believe you can do the impossible.

231

Saving Grace

They cried to the LORD in their trouble,
and he saved them from their distress.
He sent out his word and healed them;
he rescued them from the grave.

PSALM 107:19-20

Lord, I was proud, and you humbled me. I was selfish, and you showed me compassion. I was cold, and you taught me to feel. I was empty, and you filled me. I was dark, and you brought me into the light.

The power of your Word came into my being, and I have been saved. Once I looked at my life as meaningless and without purpose beyond physical and material pursuits. Now I understand that my life is one to be lived spiritually and within your grace. I was unloved, and now I am loved.

232

Laundry Day

I said, "Have mercy on me, LORD;
heal me, for I have sinned against you."

PSALM 41:4

Don't we all have dirty laundry that we hang out for other people to see? Some days I walk around littering every place I go with my spiritual dirty laundry. Is it that I do not care what people think? Or that I do not care about my spirit enough to carry my sin to you as you call me to do?

Lord, receive me and my dirty laundry today. I know it is quite a pile. I was chatting away about grace to everyone instead of actually coming to you to receive that grace. I was talking up salvation to my unsaved neighbors, while privately ignoring the urge to praise you and ask for forgiveness. And as they say, all these dirty items in my life are starting to smell to high heaven. It is definitely time for a laundry day.

233

Whole Again

*Restore to me the joy of your salvation
and grant me a willing spirit, to sustain me.*

PSALM 51:12

My joy is complete in you, Lord. The holes in my spirit created by doubt or pain are filled, and I am renewed as a believer, as a child of God. My spirit knows the hand of its Healer, and it soars in your presence. As I pray to you, my life is resurrected, and my spirit is willing and able to keep following you and your ways.

Your grace cleanses me from my past mistakes, my times of weakness or trouble, and you have made me new again. When I am reluctant to recognize this because I want to do things my way or take credit for my state of grace, my spirit reminds me that you are the faithful healer of all things past, present, and future. I am merely the vessel in need of your healing. I pray to really see myself whole and renewed, and I acknowledge your salvation and mercy.

234

Worship

*Blessed be your glorious name, and may it be exalted
above all blessing and praise. You alone are the LORD.
You made the heavens, even the highest heavens, and
all their starry host, the earth and all that is on
it, the seas and all that is in them. You give life to
everything, and the multitudes of heaven worship you.*

NEHEMIAH 9:5-6

Praise. Reverence. Vulnerability. When I take time to worship you and thank you for all that you are, I feel the longing to praise rise in my spirit. I become humble and aware of my weakness. I realize how much I need to come to you just to get through each day. I question why I would ever resist this pull toward your Spirit.

May I learn to worship you with the awe and wonder my Creator deserves. And may I leave a time of such prayer and praise with a deeper sense of how much I love the One who first loved me.

Healthy Soul

*Dear friend, I pray that you may enjoy good
health and that all may go well with you,
even as your soul is getting along well.*

3 JOHN 2

I have noticed how my efforts toward a healthy life have also enriched my soul. I am clear-thinking, brighter, more attentive to my spiritual needs. Lord, I know I complain about this body of mine, but I ask you to bless it with healing and wholeness. Where I am having physical difficulties, direct me toward the right care. Don't let me abuse my body just because I am tired of its shortcomings.

When I focus on my breath and think about the oxygen soaring through my system, I am so grateful for the intricate workings of my body. I was made by you, and I will treat your creation with kindness—inside and out.

236

Healing Toward Peace

I will bring health and healing to it;
I will heal my people and will let them enjoy
abundant peace and security.

JEREMIAH 33:6

You heal. There is no other resource in my life that offers healing. You mend my brokenness with your offer of wholeness. You remove the hurts I have been carrying around for years. Not only do you offer healing, but the new life I am given is one of abundance and great wonders.

You don't call my personal fulfillment trivial. Instead you guide me in a way that promises this fulfillment. I thank you, God, for being so gracious and giving.

Unhealthy Living

Because of your wrath there is no health in my body;
there is no soundness in my bones because of my sin.

PSALM 38:3

My sin is like a wound. When left unattended, it becomes more painful, spreads, and deepens. The damage becomes more difficult to repair. But when I come to you right away, Lord, and confess my sin, the healing begins immediately. "Freedom from sin" is no longer just a phrase or bit of head knowledge. It is a real happening in my life. I actually have the sensation of a burden removed from my spirit.

Hear my prayers, Lord. Listen to my cries of repentance. Restore the strength of my flesh, bones, and soul.

238

Good to the Bone

*Light in a messenger's eyes brings joy to the heart,
and good news gives health to the bones.*

PROVERBS 15:30

I need some good news about now, Lord. Recent days have been filled with sad news and frustrations. I haven't been able to focus and rarely get to bed on time. My spirit is restless. God, give me healing. From my flesh to my spirit, infuse my being with the power of your good news.

I hold my faith close to me during this time. I take a walk outside and let nature's cheerfulness embrace me. Your presence is everywhere. You have not left me… even as I wait for good news and restoration.

Completely Covered

*Since you excel in everything—in faith, in
speech, in knowledge, in complete earnestness
and in the love we have kindled in you—see
that you also excel in this grace of giving.*

2 CORINTHIANS 8:7

Did I honor you today, Lord? All day I was striving
to be godly when I spoke, made choices, did work,
expressed kindness, prayed—I think that covers it. Are
you proud of me for making a conscious effort to walk
in your ways?

Now when I am here with you, recapping the day
and trying to get a report card summary out of you,
I realize how ineffective and faithless this thinking is.
You have not called me to be perfect; you have called
me to be covered by your perfect grace.

240

Gladness

Let all who take refuge in you be glad;
let them ever sing for joy.
Spread your protection over them,
that those who love your name may rejoice in you.

PSALM 5:11

have many blessings, yet my spirit leans toward sorrow or frustration so naturally. Guide me to the refuge of your mercy, Lord. When I know I am covered by you and cared for by you, I embrace gladness.

My spirits are lifted when I am in fellowship with you. Calling out your name and relying on your name bring me deep joy. May I always trust in your love and comfort, and may I always step under your protection.

Special Delivery

You are my hiding place;
you will protect me from trouble
and surround me with songs of deliverance.

PSALM 32:7

I have books and cleaning supplies delivered to my home. I can order pizza or any meal I desire to be brought to my front door. But there is nothing I can do to deliver myself from the trouble that plagues me tonight. I have tried. I have prayed for you to give me the strength to do it on my own, when all along I needed the protection of your strength.

It's not easy for me to ask for comfort and help. I am stubborn and human and often conflicted with a false sense of control. Pare away these excuses, Lord. I am in great need, and only you can deliver me.

242

Life Preserver

See how I love your precepts;
preserve my life, LORD, in accordance with your love.

PSALM 119:159

Forgive me, God. I give my heart away too easily to things of the world. It is smudged from such insincerity. It has cracks from moments of mishandling. Cleanse my heart, Lord. I want it to be shiny enough to reflect your goodness. Mend the broken places, if you will. I long to feel the beating of a whole heart once again.

Renew a spirit of honesty and integrity in me, Lord. I know how precious I am to you. Don't let me waste that kind of love on trivial pursuits or quests that end in heartbreak. My life is transformed and preserved by your love.

243

Where I End

Do not withhold your mercy from me, LORD;
may your love and faithfulness always protect me.

PSALM 40:11

Lord, where my human strength ends, your eternal might begins. Where my limited view of love and compassion stops seeing the needs around me, your love and compassion continue, revealing and covering the needs that arise. I feel so safe knowing that I do not have to be God in this relationship. There are earthly relationships where I try to play this grand role and fail miserably. But you do not ask me to be mighty and all-powerful. You ask me to run to your mercy and your truth because once I am there, I am saved from the falseness of self-reliance.

Take me into the fold of your love and give me the peace of complete surrender.

244

Return to You

The God of all grace, who called you to his eternal glory in Christ, after you have suffered a little while, will himself restore you and make you strong, firm and steadfast. To him be the power for ever and ever. Amen.

1 PETER 5:10-11

I am gathering my wounds, my weaknesses, and my worries and bringing them to you. It is quite a load. The experiences I have had with suffering created baggage…things that seem to cause me to stumble even now. I thought dragging around evidence of my past mistakes was a sign of strength. They are a heavy burden, and now I realize that I will never be strong until I release them to your grace.

Receive this stuff of my life. Restore me with your strength and mercy. Now that I won't be spending my time moving emotional baggage from here to there and back again, I will be able to serve you better, Lord. It is a comfort and relief to return to you.

247

245

Holding On

*In your hands are strength and power to exalt
and give strength to all. Now, our God, we give
you thanks, and praise your glorious name.*

1 CHRONICLES 29:12-13

Lord, help me see through the present struggles and into the future peace you have for me. Give me the calm of this peace now, as I try to regain perspective—your perspective—to see this through. I pray that you will keep holding on to me as I try to hold on to my sense of thanksgiving and praise. Turn my thoughts from selfish regrets to generous ideas and hopes.

Your strength is my strength. When will I truly believe this and rest in your power? The ground I stand on is shaky, but the hand I hold on to is not. For that I thank you, Lord.

246

Faithfully Yours

Your word, LORD, is eternal;
it stands firm in the heavens...
Your laws endure to this day,
for all things serve you.

PSALM 119:89,91

I do not often speak in terms of faithfulness. God, open my eyes to your faithfulness. There is evidence of it all around me. May I, in turn, infuse my daily existence with this gift by following through, considering other people, and serving in this life you have given me.

Before I doubt another person or situation, let me first look at my own level of commitment. Am I faithful to this friend, this project, this effort? Show me what I can do to display commitment and to honor you with a life that is faithfully yours.

Lessons to Take Along

Teach me to do your will, for you are my God;
may your good Spirit lead me on level ground.

PSALM 143:10

look at old photos and think about how I look, what I was doing, who my friends were, and what life was like. Maybe what I should examine are the lessons you were teaching me at that stage of my life. I pray to be taught your will through the wisdom of other people and the experiences that come my way. I believe that I can learn a lot right now that will help me later on as I keep walking toward higher and more level ground.

It takes perseverance to go from the lowlands to the top of the mountain. I pray that as I piece together the times of my life from memory and wisdom, I will have a greater understanding of how perseverance is not only possible, but is a natural part of the faith journey.

248

Striving for Strong Faith

Make every effort to add to your faith goodness; and to goodness, knowledge; and to knowledge, self-control; and to self-control, perseverance; and to perseverance, godliness; and to godliness, brotherly kindness; and to brotherly kindness, love.

2 PETER 1:5-7

like to add onto my online shopping cart. When standing in line at the store, I am the first to add a point-of-purchase item to my basket. Anytime I play a game, I always want to be the one to gain an extra point for the win. But Lord, I realize how little I have added to my faith lately. I discover in your Word so many qualities you hope I will desire. You reveal what a person with a godly heart desires and represents.

Hear my prayer, Lord. I want my eyes to be opened to opportunities for spiritual growth. I pray to add to my faith so that I multiply the spiritual fruit of my life's harvest.

The Greater Good

*It is God who works in you to will and to
act in order to fulfill his good purpose.*

PHILIPPIANS 2:13

The other day I felt you move within me. I was ready
to denounce my responsibility. I was ready to distance myself from a commitment. And you prodded
my soul to act wisely and in a godly way. I didn't fully
understand it at the time, but I see now that you were
leading me toward a higher purpose.

Just when I think all circumstances come down to
what I want versus what other people want, you step in
and remind me that there is indeed a good purpose to
be fulfilled. I thank you for this new perspective. May
I be aware of how the greater purpose affects the faith
of those around me. Work in me. Work through me.
Lord, use me as you wish.

250

Remaining

Brothers and sisters, each person, as responsible
to God, should remain in the situation
they were in when God called them.

1 CORINTHIANS 7:24

I want to shed my current situation. But I know you have called me to be here. This "now" I am experiencing is within your will. I sense that when I pray for release. You ask me to be patient, willing, and open.

I am overwhelmed by responsibilities I juggle in life. Ordering their priority is not simple. Help me realize that I don't have to understand how all these pieces fit together in a master plan. My only responsibility is to you. My commitment to rest in my current situation is an act of faith. I follow your call and hold on to the hope of things to come.

Working Toward Maturity

*Let perseverance finish its work so that you may
be mature and complete, not lacking anything.*

JAMES 1:4

That problem I neglected to give over to you has cir-
cled back to me again. While I did not bring it to you,
I did toss it into the cosmos, and I thought it would
sort of drift forever. Well, it is here now for a return
engagement. Lord, help me give this to you once and
for all. Then give me strength to learn the lesson of
perseverance.

I require so much work, Lord, and yet you continue to provide me with what I need, when I need it.
I never lack for anything. I am grateful for the times
when you called me to wait, to learn, to push through
a situation. You patiently work in my life so that I may
become complete in you.

252

Strength in Obedience

She sets about her work vigorously;
her arms are strong for her tasks.

PROVERBS 31:17

God, let me dive into the tasks I have before me at work and at home. I want to face my responsibilities with great strength and effort. I want to be hardworking in every setting. May my focus be to serve you, no matter what the job. When I honor you with the labor of my hands and mind, I know it strengthens me spiritually. Everything is connected to what is good and right.

Lead me to responsibilities that are of importance to you. Guide me away from fruitless efforts. I want my life to count. I want my work to please you.

253

Misplaced Trust

*You have let go of the commands of God
and are holding on to human traditions.*

MARK 7:8

God, I want to resist the temptation to hold on to the ways of mankind. Early in my faith, I reached for and grasped your teachings. I let them sink into my spirit and fill me with knowledge and light. Now as I ride the merry-go-round of life, I am tempted by the brass rings of easy solutions. I reach for them instead of your precepts.

It is difficult to turn from old habits. I set my sights on those who appear successful in life and try to follow them. Help me release my grip on the world and its truth, Lord. Inspire me to hold on to your commands with all my heart.

254

Reaching for Faith

*Timothy, my son, I am giving you this instruction
in keeping with the prophecies once made about you,
so that by recalling them you may fight the battle
well, holding on to faith and a good conscience.*

1 TIMOTHY 1:18-19

Lead me in your instruction today, God. Let me clearly feel your direction as I work and make choices. Maybe you will lead someone to speak words of truth into my life. I have received encouragement and wisdom through friends and even strangers in the past. Do not let me feel alone in my efforts. Direct me toward the fellowship of other believers. Let them counsel me in your way. I will hold on to my faith tightly today, Lord, and wait upon your wisdom.

255

Letting Go of Nothing

Hold on to instruction, do not let it go;
guard it well, for it is your life.

PROVERBS 4:13

When I filter out needless information from my gathering of knowledge, what remains are the eternal truths you provide. In my busyness, I acquire a lot of worthless detail about so many different things. I memorize addresses, PIN codes, passwords, airport regulations, and word processing shortcuts. There is little room left for your instruction.

Clear my mind, Lord. Details are important, but when I come to you in prayer, I want to let go of these bits of nothingness. Let them fade away so I can hold tightly to your instruction as you speak it into my heart.

256

The Strength of Jesus

*Christ is faithful as the Son over God's house.
And we are his house, if we hold on to our
confidence and the hope in which we glory.*

HEBREWS 3:6

am weak but he is strong." Yes, Jesus loves me. And I am so thankful. My weakness is more apparent all the time. I should be old enough to know better...about everything. But I don't. I take false steps in strange directions. I strive to measure up to the world's expectations. But what I really want is to measure up as a child of God who needs the help of her Lord. I want your power in my life.

Help me turn my hope into true strength. I am weak. But I know the One who lifts me above my circumstances. Let courage grow from my active faith.

Worst-Case Scenario

*In the morning you will say, "If only it were evening!"
and in the evening, "If only it were morning!"*

DEUTERONOMY 28:67

The flip-flop of worry turns my thoughts, my stomach, and my hope upside down. Instead of standing firm in your promises, I waver back and forth, uncertain of what I want or need. All day I long for the quiet and solitary nature of night. At night I am glad for your presence and the soothing calm before sleep overcomes my concerns.

Lord, speak to my soul. Grant me the wisdom and faith to see that there is no place or time or situation that will distance me from your sight or your peace.

258

Missing Out

*As evening approached, the disciples came to him
and said, "This is a remote place, and it's already
getting late. Send the crowds away, so they can go
to the villages and buy themselves some food."*

MATTHEW 14:15

planned and replanned my day today. Yet there were
surprises at every turn. Some were blessings, some I
hope were blessings in disguise…but they all disrupted
my big plans. I like to be efficient, Lord. When things
closed in on me, I became anxious about the outcome.

But just as you showed the disciples time after time,
there is no need to worry. Things are in your control.
When I worry, I lose sight of the purpose in that very
moment. Help me see your hand in everything that
happens—including the detours.

Choke Hold

*The seed falling among the thorns refers to
someone who hears the word, but the worries
of this life and the deceitfulness of wealth
choke the word, making it unfruitful.*

MATTHEW 13:22

I want a faith that flourishes, Lord. I want to hear your
promises and take hold of them and believe in them.
But when my worries about money, relationships, or
the day's agenda kick in, my faith suffers. My fears
stunt its growth, and I am left feeling empty.

Let me be encouraged by other believers and
uplifted by creation's wonder. Hope creates a fertile
ground where faith can take root and blossom. Guide
me toward those people and practices that will inspire
me to live a fruitful, abundant life.

260

Out and In

[The LORD] will never let the righteous be shaken.

PSALM 55:22

After talking to a friend about a problem, I can sit in my favorite chair with my favorite blanket and dissect the problem further. I can go for a long walk. Whatever mode of processing I choose leads me to a list of possible solutions. Yet nothing seems remarkable enough to work, so I keep worrying. Then I seek your Word, Lord, and am reminded to cast my cares on you. I wish it didn't take me so long to come around to your truth.

When I want someone to take my problem away, help me to pause and appreciate the better offer you make. Your promise is to walk with me, to sustain me, to hold me up as I make my way through this in your strength. You pull me out of the despair and promise to never let me fall.

261

Spare Me

*Lord my God, I called to you for help,
and you healed me.
You, Lord, brought me up from the realm of the dead;
you spared me from going down into the pit.*

PSALM 30:2-3

A flippant teenager might say, "Spare me" when they want to skip to something better. No doubt I have said "Spare me the details" or "Spare me the boring lecture" at numerous moments in my life. It's funny how the meanings of those words change after experiencing hardship. "Spare me" is not something I say now to squelch a conversation; it is what I say to start many conversations with you.

Lord, pull me from my despair, worries, and the depths of my self-pity. Place me on new heights so that I can stand tall and gain perspective once again of the life you have given to me. Spare me from the fate of my own demise. Help me.

262

Come and Get Me

I have strayed like a lost sheep.
Seek your servant, for I have not
forgotten your commands.

Psalm 119:176

As a human, I love to be found. To be found is to belong to another person or to a group or to a community. To be found is to be loved and known. God, I have strayed to a place that is far from your hand and your way. And I know that only through your grace do I have the ability to ask this one more time: Please come and get me. Find me, Lord. Help me return to the place of your presence.

Your commands are written upon my heart. Though I have strayed, I have never lost my faith in your Word and your love. Seek me out, Lord. Find me. It is to you that I want to belong forever.

Protection

*Then Jacob prayed, "O God of my father Abraham,
God of my father Isaac, LORD, you who said to
me, 'Go back to your country and your relatives,
and I will make you prosper,' I am unworthy of all
the kindness and faithfulness you have shown your
servant...But you have said, 'I will surely make
you prosper and will make your descendants like
the sand of the sea, which cannot be counted.'"*

GENESIS 32:9-10,12

God, you provide a secure way for me to head into today and the future days of my life. When I stumble, you offer your hand and lead me through the situation. I have learned faith through the act of perseverance. And I have discovered hope on the other side. Lead me, Lord. Guard my heart from becoming hardened or untrusting. I turn my fragile spirit over to your care, for you are my Father, my Maker, and my Protector.

264

Not Me, Lord

*When evening came, Jesus was reclining at the table
with the Twelve. And while they were eating, he
said, "I tell you the truth, one of you will betray
me." They were very sad and began to say to
him one after the other, "Surely not I, Lord?"*

MATTHEW 26:20-22

Under the cloak of darkness, it is easy to lie. It is
easy to even tell myself half-truths when I am certain that I can stay protected by the veil of shadows.
Thoughts that would seem impossible during the cheer
of day now flood my mind and weigh me down.

Lord, turn my negativity into an opportunity for
healing. In the past I have said, "Surely not I, Lord…"
But now I know how vulnerable I am. I will tell
myself and you the truth: I cannot overcome my self-
deception with self-talk. I need you and your light to
be present.

265

My Worth

I am poor and needy,
and my heart is wounded within me.
I fade away like an evening shadow;
I am shaken off like a locust.

PSALM 109:22-23

have been comparing myself to others again. Yes, this is a road I have taken many times. Why can't I learn to place my value solely in you rather than in the fickle preferences of the world? I don't earn enough, have enough, know enough...I am not enough when I stand alone.

Only you can shine light upon my beauty. My goodness exists because I have placed my faith in who you are. I will never be perfect by comparison to an ever-changing list of worldly requirements. But I will always be wealthy, I will have abundance, and I will be enough when I rest in your purpose for my life.

266

The Light Show

You, LORD, are my lamp;
the LORD turns my darkness into light.

2 SAMUEL 22:29

A friend reminded me of how far I have come. They knew me back when I had sorrow and emptiness. Now they notice the light that burns from within. They remember me when I was eager to turn a good moment into a gripe session and when I felt encouraged by another's discouragement.

You have turned the direction of my heart, my feet, my mind, and my actions. Since I have known you, the frown of yesterday rarely crosses my countenance. Even when trials are on the horizon, I know to follow the light of your way. And you take me far.

267

Looking for Light

He has blocked my way so I cannot pass;
he has shrouded my paths in darkness.

JOB 19:8

Dusk covers the road ahead. Different colors are cast against the sky as though a new artist were on shift. I squint, trying to see what usually is clear on the horizon.

I know it is time to get home because soon there will be no light to ease my journey. My soul craves more light. You have shrouded my path in darkness. I cannot continue with my own vision, but must trust your sight to lead me through to tomorrow's dawn.

268

First, Praise

Give glory to the LORD your God
before he brings the darkness,
before your feet stumble
on the darkening hills.

JEREMIAH 13:16

Thank you for today, Lord! I praise your name and give you the glory for all that was accomplished. May you look at what this servant has done and call it good and right. Today was not easy, but I kept hold of your Word and my path was secured.

I know the darkness will come. There will be a time when I have trials that pull me from the path and cast me onto the rocky terrain of uncertainty and risk. On this slope I will hold on to my faith—a faith that has been strengthened through my days of praise.

269

Sins of Shadows

The eye of the adulterer watches for dusk;
he thinks, "No eye will see me,"
and he keeps his face concealed.

JOB 24:15

There are those who seek anonymity as shadows create hiding places ideal for concealing sins—from human eyes. May I never allow the appearance of clouds during times of trial to become my excuse to betray you, Lord.

In faith, there is never an absence of light. Total darkness will not conceal my wrongdoings. Reveal to me any part of my life that has been left to the shadows. Give me the courage to bring indiscretions to you with a spirit of repentance and sorrow so that I never boast with pride that I have kept something from you.

270

Bright with Belief

When you ask, you must believe and not doubt,
because the one who doubts is like a wave of
the sea, blown and tossed by the wind.

JAMES 1:6

Illuminate the answers, Lord. Convict my spirit and turn me in the direction of clarity and truth. I have doubted in the past, and it made for a very bumpy voyage. When I stare out at the horizon, I want to believe there is a way through the storm. Doubt is a clouding of the mind and heart, and it disturbs any chance I have to navigate with faith.

When I ask for direction and your beacon shines to guide me, may I never look back to the dark waves behind me. Anchor my belief in the sureness of the shore that is your purpose and hope.

271

Something Remarkable

Everyone was amazed and gave praise to God. They were filled with awe and said, "We have seen remarkable things today."

LUKE 5:26

Lord, I confess I have been thinking about how unremarkable my life is. I wake up, I go to work, I try to be a good friend and a loving member of my family, but nothing extraordinary takes place. It is just me, moving through the daily necessities.

Lord, forgive me…I have forgotten how remarkable it is to breathe in and out, to be alive. Somehow, I have ignored the privilege of true joy. And how many times have I been amazed by your compassionate covering of my hurts? Each day that I move deeper into the future you have planned for me is a miracle of renewal. Praise you, Lord, for you are doing remarkable things in my life today. Sometimes I need to be reminded.

272

Tell the World

Everyone living in Jerusalem knows they have performed a notable sign, and we cannot deny it. But to stop this thing from spreading any further among the people, we must warn them to speak no longer to anyone in this name.

ACTS 4:16-17

So many around the world and throughout history have tried to silence your name, Lord. But your name and the gospel of salvation continue to reach across continents and into the hearts of people. I think of your disciples, who were asked not to discuss the miracles performed through your power. They were warned and threatened, yet they said they could not help speaking about all they had seen and heard. They faced risk and still remained true to you.

I thank you for freedom to share my faith. I can talk about the miraculous love I have experienced. Encourage me to use this blessing. Give me the courage to be a disciple who refuses to silence the sound of a miracle.

273

Because I Believe

*Does God give you his Spirit and work
miracles among you by the works of the
law, or by believing what you heard?*

GALATIANS 3:5

Lord, I believe you and I believe in you. This is my foundation as I read about your miracles in Scripture. But the power behind such wonders is more than people of that day or our day can fathom. God, I acknowledge that I too want to place the works of your hand up against the laws of man and nature and scrutinize them. Just a little.

Even today, I read of miraculous moments that are evidence of your work—and I must first fight the urge to see if there is another explanation. Help me to believe what I hear and read. Give me discernment in such matters so I can fully embrace the signs of your Spirit at work today.

274

Climate Control

He did not do many miracles there
because of their lack of faith.

MATTHEW 13:58

Lord, heal me from my disbelief. A climate of faith welcomes your wonders. Has my lack of faith kept you from performing a miracle in my life? It is hard for me not to be cynical sometimes. I start by being frustrated about the condition of the world, my city, my family, or my self—then, I let these feelings bleed over into my faith. Do not let me taint my spirit any further, Lord.

Restore in me a faithful heart, Lord. Lead me to people who are encouragers and who counter the apathy that builds up in my daily life. I pray that I can also be that person for others. I want to be overflowing with faith. I want to be ready to notice and shine the light on your many miracles.

Certain of Your Protection

*Have no fear of sudden disaster
or of the ruin that overtakes the wicked,
for the LORD will be at your side
and will keep your foot from being snared.*

PROVERBS 3:25-26

The world feels out of control, God. I watch the news and turn away. But later, the fear of ruin, or violence, or disaster seeps into my soul. I am awakened by the pounding of my heart. While my daily routine finishes, I am anxious and unsettled. Lord, help me to place my confidence in you. I long for the peace you offer.

When I look to you, my spirit is soothed. Replace the list of dangers that runs through my mind with words of assurance. Let me witness your hand on my life and in all circumstances. Turn my scattered worries into passages of prayer. When I see the world's pain, may I not use your protection as a reason for isolation. Let me tap into your love for empathy, compassion, and prayers of "Thy will be done."

276

Seeing the Glorious

I pray that the eyes of your heart may be
enlightened in order that you may know the
hope to which he has called you, the riches of his
glorious inheritance in his holy people, and his
incomparably great power for us who believe.

EPHESIANS 1:18-19

The view of the world through my eyes is obstructed by my many wants and needs. They build up and create barriers which are too high to climb and certainly too big to see around. Clear away this messiness and give my heart eyes that see the outline of hope up ahead. May a rainbow of your promises—your kept promises and those to follow—shine brightly on the horizon.

I keep walking toward this beautiful image, and I feel the power of my faith enable me to walk past troubles and obstacles as I make my way toward what I know to be your glory.

277

Inspire Me

*We remember before our God and Father
your work produced by faith, your labor
prompted by love, and your endurance
inspired by hope in our Lord Jesus Christ.*

1 THESSALONIANS 1:3

pray for inspiration and encouragement to come my
way. By staying distant from people and commitment, I have chosen to avoid the connections that could
inspire me in my faith. This journey is one that requires
the help of other people. Why do I resist that so?

God, please make me aware of those people who
act out of love, concern, and sincere hope in you. Let
their actions be examples that allow me a visible path
toward a deeper relationship with you. May I, in turn,
take notice of the times when I, too, can be a source of
inspiration to another.

278

Shying Away from Greatness

Because your sins are so many
and your hostility so great,
the prophet is considered a fool,
the inspired person a maniac.

HOSEA 9:7

want to express myself, Lord. I want to be free of all inhibitions, negative self-talk, and the fear of how other people view me. How many times have I squelched something that is of you because I did not want to be viewed as a maniac, a fool? I believe you speak to us in a language that sometimes is wild and out of the box. After all, you created the world beyond the box that we have created for ourselves.

Let me fly high with a sense of song and creation. Give me the courage to be inspired. Encourage in me the blossoming of more ideas, more adventures, and more life.

279

Mercy

Have mercy on me, O God,
according to your unfailing love;
according to your great compassion
blot out my transgressions.
Wash away all my iniquity
and cleanse me from my sin.

PSALM 51:1-2

Oh, have mercy on me, Lord! Let your unfailing love and great compassion rain down on my spirit. Order all that is not of you to fall away from my life. Call out the sin and rid my heart from all that is dark. Let the sea of your grace wash over my iniquities. Only your mercy brings peace to my spirit and grace to my life.

280

Traveling Together

May the God who gives endurance and encouragement give you the same attitude of mind toward each other that Christ Jesus had, so that with one heart and one voice you may glorify the God and Father of our Lord Jesus Christ.

ROMANS 15:5-6

Lord, I have figured out that the people I call friends, and those who rub me the wrong way, and those I love more than life itself...they are all fellow travelers. And as we each try to find our footing to take a step forward, we learn to depend on these other folks. What better way to inspire strength and perseverance and unity than to encourage other people on the journey.

Right now I feel strong and able to give to people besides myself. I lift up your name and know your strength is behind my words. When my body grows weary and the weight of life is too much for me, I pray that another traveler will offer me the spirit of unity and fellowship with words that come from you, just in time to inspire me to continue.

281

He Hears Me

*This is the confidence we have in approaching God: that
if we ask anything according to his will, he hears us.*

1 JOHN 5:14

Lord, thank you for hearing me. Your ears are open
to the musings of my heart, the longings of my
soul, and the questions of my mind. There is nobody
else in my life who promises to hear every part of me.
Even in my most insecure moments, I utter words
I know will reach your heart. I dwell on worries my
friends would not take seriously. I have fears that,
brought up in daily conversation, would sound unrea-
sonable. Yet, you listen.

It is a gift to be vulnerable with the Creator. You
are my Master, yet I can come to you with the simplest
needs or concerns. As your child, I seek your will and
your response. As my Father, you listen.

282

Without Shame

*Now, dear children, continue in him, so that
when he appears we may be confident and
unashamed before him at his coming.*

1 JOHN 2:28

Purify me, Lord. My sinful ways build up pride and lead me to worship idols of money, status, and success. I have tried to hide my blemishes, my stains, but that is a false life. I want the life you have laid out for me. It is spotless and clean. It is a life to honor.

As you work out your purpose in me, may I never be boastful or arrogant. This detracts from you, the Source of my confidence—and others will not understand that you are the Master of all that is good in my life. Let my mouth be quick to praise your grace, which has removed my shame, healed my wounds, and made me whole.

283

Yesterday Offers Faith for Today

You have kept your promise to your servant David
my father; with your mouth you have promised and
with your hand you have fulfilled it—as it is today.

1 KINGS 8:24

Lord, your faithfulness is so evident when I look at my life today. I still have my list of things I want to achieve or of the flaws I hope to turn over to you, but just look at how far I have come. When I look back on my past struggles, I see how you lifted me out of my trench of doubt. You told me I mattered because I was your own. You also didn't let me settle, when settling seemed so acceptable. I just wanted a little bit of relief, and you were offering complete healing. How limited my perspective is!

Today affirms all that I know about you, because in the clarity of hindsight there is not a bit of doubt. May my today be a testimony to your grace, which is so evident when I survey my yesterdays.

284

Power in the Message

They did not believe the women, because their words seemed to them like nonsense.

LUKE 24:11

When people question my message of your grace, they call my words nonsense. They are ignoring the possibility of miracles in their own lives, and it saddens me. I can only imagine how it saddens your heart. Sometimes my words are discarded before their meaning can be taken in…because I am a woman.

I am made in your image. I carry in my heart a secret that is meant to be shared. Your love overcomes the deafness of ignorance, so I will continue to share the good news. And when my gender or my presentation of your message causes it to be written off as nonsense, I will stand tall in your confidence in me and keep on trying.

Resting in Confidence

*His master replied, "Well done, good and faithful
servant! You have been faithful with a few
things; I will put you in charge of many things.
Come and share your master's happiness!"*

MATTHEW 25:23

I thank you for the many things on my plate right now.
I am able to help people. I work to create a good home.
I serve you and your church with my gifts. You are so
faithful, Lord. You have affirmed me and my current
direction by blessing me with worthwhile responsibilities and opportunities.

I am finding fulfillment, thanks to your guidance.
I am more certain of myself, and my confidence in you
grows with each passing day. When I finish a busy day
and feel good, strong, and peaceful, I sense your reassuring words: "Well done."

286

Just Ask and Believe

*If you believe, you will receive
whatever you ask for in prayer.*

MATTHEW 21:22

believe. I do, Lord. And I have a whole list of things to ask for. Lately I have been slack in numerous areas. It is because I let insecurities take over my identity in you. What a shame that is! All I need to do is ask you for guidance, perseverance, wisdom, and peace for my circumstances. You affirm my faith when you answer such prayers.

In the days ahead I will look for greater confidence and security to replace my weaknesses. I will watch for evidence of your power in my life. I have been here before and know of your faithfulness. As your promises unfold, the glory will be yours.

Speak Up, Show Up

Speak up for those who cannot speak for themselves,
for the rights of all who are destitute.
Speak up and judge fairly;
defend the rights of the poor and needy.

PROVERBS 31:8-9

Lord, I pray for the many people who struggle to make ends meet: the families who face a life of shelters and job-searching, the mothers who care for their children and sacrifice their own health and well-being. Lord, pour out your mercy on your children living in poverty and fear of the future.

Help me reach out to ease the burden of another person. Am I looking closely at those people within my very reach? Who needs assistance? When I have so much, let me multiply the blessings you give to me by extending them to other people. Your plan is not for a few to prosper. Allow me the willingness to be a steward of kindness and wealth. It is all about speaking up and showing up for your children in need.

288

Peace Offering

The fruit of that righteousness will be peace;
its effect will be quietness and confidence forever.

ISAIAH 32:17

Lord, the blessing of a righteous life is peace. How I crave to have peace in my days! You know me. I tend to worry or turn situations into complications. But when my thoughts are purely about you and your will, my heart is calmed, my soul soothed.

Still my spirit today. Breathe new confidence into my mind and walk me toward the future with confidence. You renew me in righteousness and lead me to a place of peace and effectiveness.

289

The Power of God's Voice

Can you raise your voice to the clouds
and cover yourself with a flood of water?
Do you send the lightning bolts on their way?
Do they report to you, "Here we are"?

JOB 38:34-35

I can scream at tragedy, and it will not dissipate. I can shout at my wounds from past hurts, yet they will not heal. Lord, only when I call out to you, and you in turn speak to my life, can such things happen. My voice is meant to praise you; it is not meant to hold the power of God.

Lord, right now, my personal pain takes my breath away. I can only whisper to you. The words I lift up are praises. In the midst of my trial, praises bring me into your presence. And there my soul is healed.

290

Wise Move

Does not wisdom call out?
Does not understanding raise her voice?

PROVERBS 8:1

I try to be a good leader, Lord. I seek your assistance when faced with decisions, and I pray about my every step. Please let my words be filled with your wisdom. It can be intimidating to lead other people when I do not have the right words and the right time.

When I turn to you before speaking out, you give me understanding. And wisdom calls out. I rely on you to be my voice. In my desire to lead, Lord, let my life be an expression of your message of love.

291

Cry for Help

The righteous cry out, and the LORD hears them;
he delivers them from all their troubles.

PSALM 34:17

As I go about my day, I talk to you, Lord. You hear my every mumble. You pay attention to me even when I am ranting and raving. I ask for what I think I want. I insist that things change to suit my mood. Through it all, you still love me. You know I am finding my way. Lord, forgive me when I bring you my troubles, yet neglect to say what is truly on my heart. Lord, I need you as desperately as I need air to breathe. Because you hear my cries, you turn lamentations into praises.

292

A Confident Life

The Spirit God gave us does not make us timid,
but gives us power, love and self-discipline.

2 TIMOTHY 1:7

When I approach situations that make me nervous, I focus on your Spirit of power that resides within me. My timid days are behind me because I have your strength as my foundation. Lord, give me a boldness I have never known. Let me step out with security in you.

Life will be new and different as I make decisions, communicate, and walk forward with this power. I will practice self-discipline and express love through my actions so that you, Lord, may use this new confidence for good.

Certainty

*Act with courage, and may the L*ORD
be with those who do well.

2 CHRONICLES 19:11

Fill me with courage, Lord. The confidence I receive from my worldly support is not strong. It wavers according to my current level of influence or popularity. It takes very little for my hopes to be dashed. I long to feel certain of myself and my life. I don't want opinions of other people to sway me from my known path.

I will keep my eyes upon you, Lord. Your love is my assurance. My faith and my salvation are certain. The confidence I have in these matters will lead to my success.

294

God Is with Me

Be strong and courageous, and do the
work. Do not be afraid or discouraged, for
the LORD God, my God, is with you.

1 CHRONICLES 28:20

think life is requiring too much work, Lord. I have
tried all this time to be strong, but I am slipping backward. How can I keep up? Please help me continue
through my trials when I don't have the energy to keep
going. Break my stubborn spirit so I learn to lean upon
your strength.

I can do all things when I walk with you. I pray to
be open to the work ahead. Let me not cower when
you call on me to put forth great effort. It will not
be unbearable. It will be the beginning of something
miraculous.

295

Shine Forth

Commit your way to the LORD;
trust in him and he will do this:
He will make your righteous reward shine like the dawn,
your vindication like the noonday sun.

PSALM 37:5-6

Draw me to a life of commitment, Lord. Show me where I have sin that keeps me from embracing unconditional faith. I trust you with my eternity, so why is it difficult to turn over my here and now? Release me from fear and show me the life you have planned for me. I rise up and accept all that you are doing in my life. Let my righteousness shine through even the darkest days. I will move forward as your love warms me like the sun and prepares my heart for a great harvest.

296

Never Ending

May our Lord Jesus Christ himself and God our
Father, who loved us and by his grace gave us eternal
encouragement and good hope, encourage your hearts
and strengthen you in every good deed and word.

2 THESSALONIANS 2:16-17

My ability to be optimistic seems to be limited. I spark joy for about half a day, determined to be a great Christian representative to the world, and then I falter. I stumble. I mumble. Oh, how I must seem so inconsistent. God, I want your encouragement, your hope, and your peace to be evident in my life, even when my human attempts at optimism fade or the caffeine wears off. Give me a light from within that encourages other people.

The idea of eternal, forever, and never-ending encouragement and hope becomes a foundation on which to build a life. When I do falter or fall flat on my face, I pray to draw from this never-ending hope. May my words and actions be buoyed up once again.

What Keeps Me Going

May you have mercy on me, LORD;
raise me up, that I may repay them.
I know that you are pleased with me,
for my enemy does not triumph over me.
Because of my integrity you uphold me
and set me in your presence forever.

PSALM 41:10-12

Knowing that you exist keeps me going. When I doubt all other things around me or face troubles that seem impossible to overcome, your presence keeps me sane. I pray for your mercy today, that you will find it right and good to lift me up out of this current circumstance.

I follow your precepts, Lord. I seek your heart and wisdom. Please keep me close, in the warmth of your presence, so that I do not lose sight of what is to come. Encourage me with glimpses of triumph and peace. I can hold on to these until that day of success is mine to live.

298

Permanent Press

*Not that I have already obtained all this, or have
already arrived at my goal, but I press on to take
hold of that for which Christ Jesus took hold of me.*

PHILIPPIANS 3:12

I love having a mission, Lord. Your love motivates me
to press on and take hold of all this life offers. I want
to see every opportunity you place before me. Give me
a heart large enough to take in every ounce of compassion and joy and pain intended for my journey.

Give me the strength to quit being motivated by a
drive to be perfect. Lord, my perfection is through you.
You've taken hold of me. Don't let go. You are always
the reason I press on.

299

Hunger

Blessed are those who hunger and thirst for
righteousness, for they will be filled.

MATTHEW 5:6

have friends who are hungry only for love…or for something that resembles it. They never get their fill. They chase after it like it will save them. I admit there have been times I thought this to be true. But when I met you, I understood where my hunger came from. It was so much deeper than a need for food, for people, for status.

The satisfaction I receive from your love cannot be taken away. The gratitude I feel knowing you created me just as I am is not an illusion. The wonder I feel when I seek you and your righteousness fills me and will never subside.

300

Driven by Dollars

*Keep your lives free from the love of money and be
content with what you have, because God has said,
"Never will I leave you; never will I forsake you."*

HEBREWS 13:5

want so much. And my motivation is not always a
good one. It is enticing to gather, store, and acquire
more. I find myself wanting to give over to this longing. Release me from the hold of stuff and the desire
for stuff. A lot of good can be done with money, but it
is the love of it that destroys people, nations, relationships, and the spirit.

When I find my heart lusting for the material world,
remind me of your love. No money can replace your
presence and promises in my life. And if I am tempted
to give myself over to self-serving behavior, remind me
whom I truly serve.

301

Wholehearted

Whatever you do, work at it with all your heart, as working for the Lord, not for human masters, since you know that you will receive an inheritance from the Lord as a reward. It is the Lord Christ you are serving.

COLOSSIANS 3:23-24

I want to give you my all, Lord. Fill me with the energy and hope I need to live this life fully. When days seem meaningless or my efforts useless, revive me with a sense of purpose and passion.

May I see each day as a new opportunity to show you my love and my commitment. Free me from regret so that I can accept the inheritance of abundant life. You are my inspiration and my source of motivation to follow through with the plans you place on my heart.

302

Every Part of Me

"Love the Lord your God with all your heart and with all your soul and with all your mind." This is the first and greatest commandment.

MATTHEW 22:37-38

I can count on my fingers the times I have given 100 percent. How sad is that? I want to be the person who gives more than that to you on a regular basis. Help me discover what the passionate and compassionate life can lead to.

Give me a heart for your heart. Better yet, I will give you my heart, my soul, and my mind so that I am fully yours. Your call to follow the greatest commandment will be what carries me through the days when I am tempted to settle for less.

303

Out My Window

*They will speak of the glorious splendor of your
majesty—and I will meditate on your wonderful
works. They will tell of the power of your awesome
works—and I will proclaim your great deeds.*

PSALM 145:5-6

The splendor of your majesty and might can be seen
out my window. Your glorious creation sways in the
breeze and follows the seasons guided by your plan.
Every part of nature speaks of your wonder. When I am
feeling insignificant, I glance beyond the curtains and
realize I am part of your awesome works. You included
me in your plan for this world.

Give me the spark of passion I need to proclaim
your great deeds. May I become like the majestic trees,
sure and brilliant, so that my life might speak of your
love even when words cannot be found.

304

Taking My Cues

This is how we know that we love the children of God:
by loving God and carrying out his commands. In
fact, this is love for God: to keep his commands.

1 JOHN 5:2-3

Passion is considered many things in today's culture. As a believer, I understand passion to be a combination of commitment and effort to follow your heart. Ignite the desire in me to serve others and to seek out the best for those in my life. Create in me a heart that is on fire with your love and compassion for others.

I know I will still question you sometimes because I will be afraid of the risk involved in loving your children. But I believe a bigger and better life awaits the person who obeys and cherishes your commands.

305

You Alone

Hezekiah prayed to the LORD: "LORD, the God of Israel, enthroned between the cherubim, you alone are God over all the kingdoms of the earth. You have made heaven and earth."

2 KINGS 19:15

You alone formed my mind and body. You alone formed the land on which I walk and sculpted the curve of the earth. You alone know my past, present, and future. Lord and Creator, you are so worthy of praise. May my words and deeds express my love and praise to you each day.

I rule over a few scattered decisions. You are Ruler over the course of all life. I pray that I am worthy to be called yours and that my motives are always to glorify you alone—my God, my Creator, my Lord.

306

Almighty

The heavens praise your wonders, LORD,
your faithfulness too, in the assembly of the holy ones.
For who in the skies above can compare with the LORD?...
Who is like you, LORD God Almighty?
You, LORD, are mighty,
and your faithfulness surrounds you.

PSALM 89:5-6,8

The world considers mightiness to be measured in muscles and influence. But Lord, you are almighty, and your strength surpasses my human understanding of power. Since the beginning of time, your creation has bowed down before you. Who or what else can possibly compare with your grace and your authority?

Lord, you rule over all creation, and still your faithfulness is evident in my humble life. I love you because your power does not force people from your presence. The strength of your love calls people to your heart.

Let the Word Out

I will glory in the LORD;
let the afflicted hear and rejoice.
Glorify the LORD with me;
let us exalt his name together.

PSALM 34:2-3

When you listen to my speech after a long day, do you hear words that praise you, that please you? Help me to be more careful of the way I speak or express my emotions. May I be mindful that praises spoken throughout a good day or during the hard times can fall upon the ears and hearts of those who desperately want to believe in you.

By glorifying your name, I am telling other people that I am yours. I show them that when I am weak, it is your strength that pulls me through, and when I am strong, it is your love that is carrying me each step of the way.

308

Fill Me, Lead Me

I will praise the LORD, who counsels me;
even at night my heart instructs me.

PSALM 16:7

I am not afraid of the darkness that falls tonight. All day I have been waiting for it, looking forward to a special time to seek your instruction. My days are filled with many questions and decisions, so at night my heart hungers for your counsel.

Guide me, Lord. You are holy and mighty. Even while I sleep, you tell my heart about the secrets of the universe and about the wonders of your leading. How grateful I am for your voice that speaks promises and hope to my spirit every hour of the day.

Every Hour

I will extol the LORD at all times;
his praise will always be on my lips.

PSALM 34:1

Like the church hymn says, I profess that I need thee every hour, Lord. Even when I do not acknowledge that fact every moment of my day, it is true. I rely on your strength and insight and compassion. May my actions and my words and my thoughts reflect your goodness at all times.

May praise fall from my lips and rise to be heard in the heavens, Lord. And may my gratitude for the new life you offer be expressed in who I am so that others will see a reflection of you, my merciful God.

310

Who Has Loved Me

Praise be to God,
who has not rejected my prayer
or withheld his love from me!

PSALM 66:20

I have felt left alone. Forgotten. Overlooked. Unheard. I have raised my voice and my fist to the air, Lord. You remember. Caught up in my sorrow and my questions, I doubted your love. But you never left my side. You have never thrown up your hands and said, "Forget it. This person is off my list."

When I recall the times I was not praying because it hurt too much, I know that my heart was lifting up cries for love and help on my behalf. And you heard me, you heard my heart…every time. Praise be to God, for you are faithful.

311

Song for a Lifetime

I will sing to the LORD all my life;
I will sing praise to my God as long as I live.
May my meditation be pleasing to him,
as I rejoice in the LORD.

PSALM 104:33-34

No matter the time of day, I will sing praises to your name, God. I will become more aware of how I live out my faith and how I extend the grace you have extended to me. I will honor you with acts of kindness, courage, and compassion.

Each day is a new chance to display your goodness through my words and actions. Was today a pleasing offering to you, Lord? Did I step into and through all that you had for me? As I reflect on my actions and motivations, I pray that I have been a vessel of your love because I am so thankful for it in my life.

312

Promise Keeper

Lord, the God of Israel, there is no God like you
in heaven above or on earth below—you who
keep your covenant of love with your servants
who continue wholeheartedly in your way.

1 Kings 8:23

God, your promises are sacred. I build a life upon these gifts of hope. My steps have faltered over the years, but I always regain my balance when I make my way back to these promises. You keep a covenant with me even when my focus wanders away from faith. You do not deny me when I come to be in your presence.

Lord, it is in your hand that I can be free. It is under your will that I find my true path. And it is as I praise you and honor you with my life that I discover the beauty of these promises.

313

Awe

LORD, I have heard of your fame;
I stand in awe of your deeds, LORD.
Repeat them in our day,
in our time make them known;
in wrath remember mercy.

HABAKKUK 3:2

Before I knew you personally, I had friends who loved you. Even when I would challenge such belief, I was always watching for the signs of your existence. Lord, through the lens of my friends' faith, I began to see how you cared for those who put their faith in your way. I saw the gift of renewal and the impact of your influence in all that they did and said, even when they were struggling to understand you.

Lord, now I am so thankful to know you. And while I strive to define my faith and live it out for other people to see, I pray for your awesome touch to find me and my life. Let other people be in awe of the God I know.

314

Better than Life

*I have seen you in the sanctuary and beheld your
power and your glory. Because your love is better
than life, my lips will glorify you. I will praise you
as long as I live, and in your name I will lift up
my hands. I will be satisfied as with the richest of
foods; with singing lips my mouth will praise you.*

PSALM 63:2-5

found myself obsessing over the monthly bills the
other day. I went over the numbers again and again,
willing them to be different. It was not until later that
afternoon that I paid attention to all that was going
on outside my window. You had given me a beautiful day—spectacular and glorious. I was just a few feet
away from your sanctuary and a day of saying praises,
yet I had wasted time on something as temporal as bills.

Lord, I pray for soul satisfaction that does not
depend on physical comforts. Let the greatness of my
God satisfy me like an endless banquet of food and provision. May I begin each tomorrow by first approaching your heart and offering up my gratitude.

315

High Above

He also made the stars... God set them in the vault
of the sky to give light on the earth, to govern the
day and the night, and to separate light from
darkness. And God saw that it was good.

GENESIS 1:16-18

Stars twinkle beyond my reach, but not above my faith. Nothing exceeds the extent of my hope in you. When I consider the people of the world, there are too many to count. Am I not just one of your many children? How do you have time to hear my prayers, my concerns, my celebrations?

Then I consider how you made the stars. You placed them with care in the sky. There are so many—too many to count. Yet your care is evident when those night beacons shine brightly and lead me back to belief in a God who knows me intimately, personally, and who hears each prayer that leaves my lips.

316

All That I Have

Now may the God of peace…equip you with
everything good for doing his will, and may he
work in us what is pleasing to him, through Jesus
Christ, to whom be glory for ever and ever. Amen.

HEBREWS 13:20-21

It isn't much, this offering of my life, but it's all that I have to give. It isn't much, this day I have lived, but it is what I have to offer right now. My praise might not sound like the salutation of angels, but it is all my lips can form.

My heart often feels void of the compassion you possess, but it is ready to be filled by your love. My future is uncertain, but it is yours to shape. Receive these humble offerings with pleasure and grace. May you take the raw materials that make up my life and transform them into a journey and offering that serves your will and delights your heart. Even when I can't see value in one of my days or in a few of my words, I trust that you use my life for glory when I walk in your way and speak from a heart shaped by you.

317

The Song I Sing

*I will praise God's name in song
and glorify him with thanksgiving.*

PSALM 69:30

When I reach a goal, the glory is yours, Lord. When I experience a time of plenty, may words of thanksgiving pour from my lips. If I fall, stumbling because of my own blindness, I will express my thanksgiving before you help me back up. My faith is my song. My heart knows the lyrics, and my spirit whistles the tune when I need comfort.

When I look at how far I have come in my faith, I am so very grateful to belong to you, my Redeemer.

318

Your Strength

*Help us, LORD our God, for we rely on you, and in your
name we have come against this vast army. LORD, you
are our God; do not let mere mortals prevail against you.*

2 CHRONICLES 14:11

There are times when I feel there is an army just outside my front door waiting to take me down. The fear
builds up because I am focused on my strength and not
on yours. God, help me to rely on you and turn to you
even when I feel the fear building.

Do not let me fall back on my own ability when
I have the source of your might to pull me through. I
am so thankful that you do not ask me to go it alone.
When I look to you for direction and encouragement,
I have already won the battle.

319

What You Give

I gave them the words you gave me and they accepted them. They knew with certainty that I came from you, and they believed that you sent me. I pray for them. I am not praying for the world, but for those you have given me, for they are yours.

JOHN 17:8-9

When I cannot think of anything to say, please give me the words that are needed. There are people in my life who need advice, counsel, wisdom, and help. When I search my mind for the perfect thing to say, I draw a blank. I can only turn them toward you. May they see my dependence upon you so that they will have confidence in the words you give me to share.

These people are the ones I pray for most. You know them and their personal journeys, and I am thankful that you entrust them to me…people for me to know, to pray for, and to care about.

320

Leaning on Your Wisdom

God gave Solomon wisdom and very great insight, and a breadth of understanding as measureless as the sand on the seashore.

1 KINGS 4:29

My hope for wisdom is grounded in my faith in your promises. If I am left to my own devices and motivation, I will never understand the world around me. And it is not only these external mysteries I long to explore. I hope to discover more about my own heart and mind and my Creator.

I depend upon your wisdom, Lord. Free my mind of the half-truths, untruths, and misconceptions so my growth is not hindered by lies and foolishness. I pray that the way I use my gift of wisdom will reflect my thankful heart.

321

Freedom Through Dependence

If anyone acknowledges that Jesus is the Son of
God, God lives in them and they in God. And so
we know and rely on the love God has for us.

1 JOHN 4:15-16

Only you, Lord, offer me deep love. I dive in and feel your presence all around me. We are a part of one another. Creator and creation. I am so blessed to have met and accepted the gift of Christ. This relationship is sufficient for all my needs. This love has covered my iniquities. Dependence has given me freedom and a path to eternity.

When I meet someone in pain, I want them to know your love. How do they make it, if not with you? Even a life filled with blessings encounters stumbling blocks. Lord, next time I am hurt, broken, and weak, immerse me in the depths of your mercy. As I surface and struggle for air, I depend on your breath of life to fill my being.

322

I Trusted You Before I Knew You

From birth I have relied on you;
you brought me forth from my mother's womb.
I will ever praise you.

PSALM 71:6

Lord, you were there when I was formed in my mother's womb. You knew my heart, my character, my purpose as I was brought into the world. I was so defenseless then, so vulnerable. I know your hand was upon my life for every minute. Even before I had a personal relationship with you, I relied on you completely.

Now I am so established in the world and can appear strong and in control. But I confess I am as vulnerable as the day I was born. I praise you for the countless times you have protected me, saved me without my knowledge. O Lord, your loving hand was and will be with me every step of the way. I am so glad to be your child.

323

He Is My Mighty Rock

My salvation and my honor depend on God;
he is my mighty rock, my refuge.

PSALM 62:7

Lord, you tower over my life. Your presence intimidates my enemies. You are my refuge during times of trouble. When I experience days of doubt, I climb onto your rock of refuge. I stand against the wind and view my fretting from new heights. I see you crush my worries in the shadow of your strength. I need not be afraid.

You are my safe place, Lord. I rise to sit on your shoulders when I feel small. I lean against the weight of your power and restore my strength. You are my security at all times. God, my life requires your authority. I want you to reign over my days. Help me build a spirit of perseverance and a character of honor on the foundation of your goodness.

324

See My Pain

Relieve the troubles of my heart
and free me from my anguish.
Look on my affliction and my distress
and take away all my sins.

PSALM 25:17-18

Lord, see the depth of my pain. I am facing difficulties, and I feel alone as I seek solutions for my problems. Just as I put out one fire, I smell the smoke of another about to burst forth in flames. There has been so much. I don't know where to begin...except at the foot of your cross. Free me, Lord. Take my anguish and my affliction and have mercy on my soul.

These problems that are surfacing—many are caused by bad decisions made in haste and without your guidance. Forgive me, God. This isn't the first time I have been overwhelmed by trouble. Lord, give me strength. Turn to me and see the repentance in my eyes and heart.

325

The Way

*It is God who arms me with strength
and keeps my way secure.*

PSALM 18:32

I am officially on my way to becoming a mature being. I feel that I am taking care of my responsibilities. I'm managing my home, my job, and my plans. I've started thinking about the future more so I can be prepared. It feels good to be independent of others and have confidence in my decisions.

Through your strength, I can stand on the foundation of my life and look forward to all you have for me. I don't know what is going to happen tomorrow or a year from now or around the bend as my life unfolds, so I am even more thankful that you hold my future in your hands. The way ahead is perfect because it is crafted by my Creator.

326

See It All

Search me, God, and know my heart;
test me and know my anxious thoughts.
See if there is any offensive way in me,
and lead me in the way everlasting.

PSALM 139:23-24

Well, I might as well face it: By now you know me and my faults. You have seen me yell at my spouse, neglect someone who needed attention, take the easy way out to avoid commitment, etc. And these are just the faults I am willing to speak of today. The fact that you know me so well and still love me is one of life's greatest mysteries. I realize that I still try to keep my transgressions from you sometimes. I even try to keep them from myself.

But here I am, asking for you to see it all—the good, the bad—and show me what is next for me. Now that you know me, I pray to become the person you know I can be.

327

See Me, Show Me

Yet you know me, LORD;
you see me and test my thoughts about you.

JEREMIAH 12:3

I long to have the kind of connection that puts me at ease in your presence and replaces my doubts and questions with certainty. Search my ways of thinking, my pattern of emotions, and my view of the world, and repair any false perspectives I have.

God, I pray for knowledge that gives me a greater understanding of you. See me and test my thoughts about you to see if they are strong in truth. I want to know you. I pray to be open to your correction and testing. I pray to give myself over to you and your purpose. Show me how to depend on you completely.

328

Hold That Thought

You discern my going out and my lying down;
you are familiar with all my ways.
Before a word is on my tongue
you, LORD, know it completely.

PSALM 139:3-4

Thank goodness I caught some regrettable words before they left my mouth and entered the mind of another person. However, you heard what thoughts I was forming. You heard the attitude and my unwillingness to extend kindness. This is the kind of relationship we have: I seek you, and you already know me inside and out.

I pray that as my faith grows stronger and deeper, I will not have to hold back so many thoughts and words. I pray for a purer view of life and people. Give me a compassionate heart so I reach out with words of comfort and peace, rather than stinging lines of controversy or division. May my familiar ways be pleasing to you, Lord.

Thanksgiving

*Then Hannah prayed and said: "My heart rejoices
in the LORD; in the LORD my horn is lifted high. My
mouth boasts over my enemies, for I delight in your
deliverance. There is no one holy like the LORD; there
is no one besides you; there is no Rock like our God."*

1 SAMUEL 2:1-2

I rejoice in you, my Lord. I find salvation in your love
and grace. Only when I depend on you for everything am I free to experience your abundance. I pray
that when trouble or want finds me, I will not turn
from you or deny my faith. As I stand on the moun-
taintop of joy, may I remember the view and return to
this image. My praises shall fill the canyon below and
the sky above.

I hope to make gratitude my offering to you each
day. Through my speech, my actions, and my efforts,
may you know that I am so very thankful for you.

330

One of Many

Praise awaits you, our God, in Zion;
to you our vows will be fulfilled.
You who answer prayer,
to you all people will come.
When we were overwhelmed by sins,
you forgave our transgressions.

PSALM 65:1-3

know I am one of many of your creations. I know my voice is one of many that rises to be heard in this world…heard by you. My simple sin today is one of many in my lifetime…my journey covered with blemishes that undermine the beauty of the life I could be living. And even though I am one of many who praise you and call you God, you listen to every prayer that leaves my lips.

I am humbled, overwhelmed, and truly thankful for your presence in my life. When I pray, I am no longer one of many. I am the one you care for and listen to.

331

Timidity

May my supplication come before you;
deliver me according to your promise.
May my lips overflow with praise,
for you teach me your decrees.

PSALM 119:170-171

I can be shy about approaching you. Sometimes I am a young child who is not certain what to say or how to find my way through a prayer to get to the heart of the matter. But when I release my inhibitions and come to you with a humble and open spirit, my mouth overflows with all that is in me. My gratitude, my concern, my questions…they all pour forth. I am surprised by how quickly I become like a pair of open hands, waiting to receive what you give to fill me.

May my timidity turn into humility, so I do not stand on the sidelines, too nervous to approach you. I long to run to your side, bursting with courage, love, and gratitude as I tell you about my day, with no holding back.

332

The Grace of Knowing

He has shown you, O mortal, what is good.
And what does the LORD require of you?
To act justly and to love mercy
and to walk humbly with your God.

MICAH 6:8

Lord, lately I need a softer heart, a less judgmental mind, a more open spirit. I sense your leading when I am with other people, yet my very human tendencies stop me from doing what you require of me. Please give me compassionate eyes that see only the need and beauty in people. May my thoughts turn to how you wish for me to interact with someone, rather than how I want to take control of the situation.

Remind me, Lord, that justice and mercy are the cornerstones of my faith. Let me pass along these gifts to other people so that my humility becomes the source of my response to your children.

333

Gotta Dance, Gotta Sing

*You turned my wailing into dancing;
you removed my sackcloth and clothed me with joy,
that my heart may sing your praises and not be silent.*

PSALM 30:11-12

With all that you have going on, Lord, I'm amazed that you still encourage my heart to express its emotions. One day I am asking for your mercy. Another day I await your blessing for an opportunity. You do not call me to be silent. While people rarely have time to hear the thoughts of another, you lovingly wait for my life song.

When my circumstances change, I owe it all to you. It is not of my doing that rain turns to sunshine. So it is not my doing when tears are dried by true joy. Thank you, Lord.

334

Daily Sweetness

Light is sweet,
and it pleases the eyes to see the sun.
However many years anyone may live,
let them enjoy them all.

ECCLESIASTES 11:7-8

Thank you for this day. When I stepped outside and I felt the warmth of the sun on my face, I was filled with gratitude. I don't always recognize my days as gifts. They can blur together into a string of indistinguishable moments. But I am learning to enjoy my life, bit by bit.

Lord, give me a desire for my own life. Help me exchange grumblings for peaceful prayers. May I always feel the warmth of your light and celebrate each day fully.

335

Your Perfect Will

Do not conform any longer to the pattern of this world, but be transformed by the renewing of your mind. Then you will be able to test and approve what God's will is—his good, pleasing and perfect will.

ROMANS 12:2

So many choices and decisions seem to fill my world, Lord. I pray to rest in your will and your way so that I do not lose sight of my future as a child of God. My work can consume me, and my worries about material things can undermine the blessings. Change my heart, Lord. Let the matters of eternal importance become my priority list.

Oh, how I crave a life of significance. But even as I pray, a flood of insecurities can fill me, and I have no room left for the purpose you wish to pour into my cup. Let me not be anxious to fill my life with clutter and trivial distractions, Lord. Let my life, my heart, my soul be vessels that await the flow of your Spirit.

336

Release Me from Worry

My comfort in my suffering is this:
Your promise preserves my life.

PSALM 119:50

Lord, you are my source of strength in all things. How do I forget that your mighty hand is placed upon my life? Today, I give over to you the many things that occupy my mind and my heart. Help me to release my worries to you as they take hold of me. These anxieties keep me from embracing the life you have planned for me. Your mercy surrounds me with comfort. Your love is my source of strength. Your promises are my future.

Meet me today, Lord. Here in this moment. In the midst of the troubles that weigh me down. Sometimes it is difficult for me to ask for help. To admit to weakness. But my soul is weary, and I want to give my burdens over to you. You are a mighty, faithful God. Thank you, Lord. My hope for what will unfold is buoyed as my prayers are spoken.

Hope and a Future

*"I know the plans I have for you," declares the
LORD, "plans to prosper you and not to harm
you, plans to give you hope and a future."*

JEREMIAH 29:11

My to-do lists and the task reminders that pop up on my computer screen reflect a bit of my nature. Lord, I like to know what will occur and how it will take place. No surprises for me, please. I equate the unknown with potential problems. Cure me, Lord, of such a pessimistic view of my future. I have hope…I just want control too. It is so very shortsighted of me to have such little trust in you, the Creator of the world and of my life.

Reach out and still my active, worried mind so it receives and accepts your Word. You have plans to prosper me and not to harm me. Replace my anticipation of complications with assurance of security. May I start and end my to-do lists with prayers of thanksgiving.

338

Self-Talk

*I am convinced that neither death nor life, neither
angels nor demons, neither the present nor the future,
nor any powers, neither height nor depth, nor anything
else in all creation, will be able to separate us from
the love of God that is in Christ Jesus our Lord.*

ROMANS 8:38-39

I f I could have a conference call with my past self, present self, and future self, I believe I would discover one truth: Your love has always been with me. The voices of my self over the course of my life would share stories about testing your commitment. I tried to measure your love by running far from heaven's reach. I stretched your love by pushing the boundaries. I shoved away your love when my doubt tried to poke holes in your truth.

And your love remained.

I have many questions about my future, but after listening to the course of my life, one thing is certain—my heart will never be separated from the love of its Creator.

341

339

Making the Effort

Whatever your hand finds to do, do it with all your might, for in the realm of the dead, where you are going, there is neither working nor planning nor knowledge nor wisdom.

ECCLESIASTES 9:10

This is my chance. I know this. I sometimes fixate on this fact. This is my one chance at life here on earth. You have given me this earthly body, this heart for you, and the plans you conceived for my life before it ever began. I pray that my efforts are worthy in your sight, Lord. When I struggle and strain, let it be for a good cause. Let each and every effort I make be done with sincerity and honor.

Heaven's glory shimmers in the distance. I look toward it in my heart so I know the way home. But these days of living in full humanity also serve a divine purpose. I am to love you, love others, serve you, serve others, and discover who I am in the process.

340

Off Track

*There is no wisdom, no insight, no plan
that can succeed against the LORD.*

PROVERBS 21:30

I have a planner overflowing with...well, plans, of course. Each day's box lays claim to a portion of my life. I know that each time I set a commitment down in blue ink, I am also claiming a portion of the time you have planned for me. I imagine I am steering things in the wrong direction more times than not. I take great comfort in knowing you are able to guide my random efforts back to your intention for my life.

As I make plans for the days ahead, may I seek your guidance, your priorities, and your will. When I follow your direction, the meaning of each day is magnified. The possibilities to serve you become clear.

341

Desiring Your Desires

*May he give you the desire of your heart
and make all your plans succeed.*

PSALM 20:4

In a culture of trends and fads, I lose sight of the differences between what I want and what I need. I misjudge which desires are born of a passion for and from you and which are longings tied to the world's riches and temporary treasures. Have I come to expect anything and everything from your hand, Lord? My worries about "having it all" fill my prayers. Turn my heart toward a desire for righteousness and faith.

You care for my basic needs. I need not fret over the material things that flow in and out of my hands. I need not be consumed with expectations of wealth and fame. As a daughter of the King, I have the freedom to let go of such things and embrace the hope of your care.

342

The First Step

In their hearts humans plan their course,
but the LORD establishes their steps.

PROVERBS 16:9

I have great intentions, Lord. You know my heart carries with it many hopes and plans. Some have come to pass, and others I wait for with patience from you. But lately I sense my life shifting ever so slightly. One moment, my eyes are cast on a defined horizon, and in the next, they are peering at something hazy. Without my permission, without my foreknowledge, my true future emerges. You encourage my spirit to carry on.

Thank you, God, for letting me rest in the security of your plans, not my own. Things change—sometimes so quickly that I lose my footing. But as I take the first step in a new direction, I know you are holding me upright and directing each step.

343

Here I Stand

The plans of the LORD stand firm forever,
the purposes of his heart through all generations.

PSALM 33:11

Before I was born, you knew what my forever looked like. You planted seeds of purpose in my heart. Over time you nurtured those seeds and encouraged me to grow. The legacy of your faithfulness continues in my life.

I stand here today excited about what my future might bring. Each day that I draw closer to you, I better understand how your plans manifest in both simple and extraordinary ways. I am thankful that as your heir, my birthright is a future of faith.

344

On Schedule

The plans of the diligent lead to profit
as surely as haste leads to poverty.

PROVERBS 21:5

It seems like I am always comparing my life plan to that of others. I wonder if I am behind schedule for all that I hope to have or accomplish. God, forgive me for this constant and worthless use of energy. Grant me the discipline to break the habit of letting my concerns for tomorrow control my today. I want contentment that comes from trusting you. I don't want to rush into decisions that reflect what others are doing. I want to wait on your leading.

My life will unfold in the way you intended for me. There is comfort in knowing I do not need to catch up with anyone else's plan. I have a custom-made life, and I am right on schedule.

345

Excited

Trust in the LORD with all your heart
and lean not on your own understanding;
in all your ways submit to him,
and he will make your paths straight.

PROVERBS 3:5-6

Amazing! Right now I am participating in the plan you have for me. I didn't just wake up to any ordinary day—I took another step toward the future you have for me. When I flip through my mental photo album of memories, I can see how you have protected me and led me through the peaks and valleys of my journey. I submit to and commit to all that you have planned for me.

Through the power of faith, I have a purpose and my life has meaning. My hope extends beyond my today and into the future because you have made it so. I'm excited to see what you have in store.

346

Wisdom

God understands the way to [wisdom]
and he alone knows where it dwells,
for he views the ends of the earth
and sees everything under the heavens.

JOB 28:23-24

Wisdom and understanding escape most of us. We look for it in all the wrong places. But you, Lord, know the way to it. Your eyes can see the place where it dwells and where it flows through time and through creation. I pray for your wisdom. I want to carry it within me for the rest of my life.

I don't know what forever will bring, but if I live in your wisdom and your way, I trust the journey. It is in your hands, and they formed the world. How simple for you to shape my future.

Let It Be

*Do not worry about tomorrow, for
tomorrow will worry about itself.*

MATTHEW 6:34

want control over today and tomorrow. I know you
can do a much better job, Lord, but I still battle for
control. I don't have a great track record when I try to
take the reins from your hands. Let today affect my
tomorrow. Give me the strength I need in this moment
to give you my tomorrow.

There will be worries. There will be struggles. But
tomorrow is also filled with possibility. I am inching
closer to eternity, and this is a journey I want to savor,
not suffer through. Give me the courage to live fully
today and await tomorrow with great hope.

348

The Lord's Prayer

Our Father in heaven, hallowed be your name,
your kingdom come, your will be done,
on earth as it is in heaven.
Give us today our daily bread.
And forgive us our debts,
as we also have forgiven our debtors.
And lead us not into temptation,
but deliver us from the evil one.

MATTHEW 6:9-13

God in heaven and all around me, I thank you for hearing the prayers of your child. May I pray with a heart of humility that receives your will and guidance and grace without my own judgments getting in the way. Lord, grant me the sense of hope I need to truly engage in communication with my Creator. Lead me into times of open dialogue with you. Bring me to my knees so that I can be humble enough to open my mind, heart, and spirit to receive your love and to fully feel your power and glory. Amen.

Prayers for Healing

This is what the LORD, the God of your
father David, says: I have heard your prayer
and seen your tears; I will heal you.

2 KINGS 20:5

I weep in private, away from the well-meaning inquiries of friends. And you, Lord, see my tears. Awkward, shattered expressions of pain and confusion stumble from my lips, yet you heal the words. My prayer is whole when it falls upon your heart. Your answer is complete: You love me. You see me. You will heal my brokenness.

It must be difficult to explain the ways of life and loss to your children. When I ask "Why, Lord?" you do not turn away from me and my neediness. You hold me close and show your heart. It is broken too—you have taken my pain. I watch your tears fall and understand they have healed me.

350

Merciful Lord

The LORD has heard my cry for mercy;
the LORD accepts my prayer.

PSALM 6:9

I walked around numb and in denial for months, Lord. My facade was perfect. I didn't miss a beat at work. I stood in the grocery store express line and not one soul looked at me with pity. I encouraged a hurting friend with words that I myself could not yet accept about you: "You are a merciful Lord."

Then my heart spoke up. It sent out an SOS cry for mercy and compassion on my behalf. Lord, thank you for accepting this prayer. I could not gather the courage or energy to bring you my burdens. I was sick and tired of myself, but you raised me out of the trap of self-pity. I am a new creation. I accept the truth about you: You are merciful, Lord.

351

Prayer Song

*By day the LORD directs his love,
at night his song is with me—
a prayer to the God of my life.*

PSALM 42:8

sing to you, Lord. My joy, heartache, and thanksgiving create a symphony of emotion. In the solitude of nightfall, I cannot help but sing. I release the worries of my day to your care. I trust you with my today and my tomorrow. My panic turns to peace as the first notes of praise drift heavenward.

Your concern touches me. Your voice blends with mine for a few sweet moments. You wrote this song to comfort me every night. You share it with me so I can come to you when the confines of words and dialogue stifle meaning. By day, Lord, guide me with your love. By night, free me with your melody. In every moment you are the God of my life.

352

True Devotion

*Devote yourselves to prayer, being
watchful and thankful.*

COLOSSIANS 4:2

God, can you work with me on my commitment
issues? Build in me a desire to pray. I want to be a
disciplined follower. Steady my spirit to stillness. Quiet
and solitude prepare me for your presence. Direct my
eyes to be watching for your answers, watching as my
prayers are heard and responded to. I want to see and
recognize your work in my life.

Cause my faith to grow, Lord. Each day that I come
to meet with you, may I know you better. Replace my
ignorance with your knowledge. Help me be strong in
my commitment to you. Show me how to pray, Lord.

353

Praise

May my prayer be set before you like incense;
may the lifting up of my hands be
like the evening sacrifice.

PSALM 141:2

talk too much. My prayers don't leave room for breath and reflection. I petition without praise. Lord, lead me to a deeper prayer life. Even as I pray right now, I can let my mind wander to things that need to be done, or requests I want to make while I have your attention.

Let me come to you in silence and with a spirit of worship. May my words wind their way to you like tendrils of burning incense. In your presence I will surrender my insecurities and the version of what my life should be like so that you, in your wisdom and mercy, can shape my future and my heart so that they are useful and pleasing to you.

354

Prayers of Protection

*I have given them your word and the world has hated
them, for they are not of the world any more than I am
of the world. My prayer is not that you take them out of
the world but that you protect them from the evil one.*

JOHN 17:14-15

I pray today as your Son prayed for his followers. I ask
for your protection from evil while I am in the world.
Being here creates opportunity for me to share my faith,
to develop a deeper relationship with you, and to taste
the richness of the life you have given me. But I know
I am not truly of the world.

In troubled times I'm tempted to ask you to remove
my burdens or to release me from the pressure of life in
the world. But you call me to walk in the plan you have
for me. So protect me, Lord, for the rest of my days, so
I can fulfill your will.

355

Find Me Faithful

Be joyful in hope, patient in affliction,
faithful in prayer. Share with God's people
who are in need. Practice hospitality.

ROMANS 12:12-13

May my life be a living prayer to you. When I cannot find the right words, let the beating of my heart do the speaking. May my actions toward other people be a prayer of hospitality and compassion. Lord, turn my fear into patience when I face hardship so I can demonstrate the power of prayer to other people.

Your Word reveals how to be a living prayer. I will glean from its endless wisdom and apply its truths to each situation. As long as there is need in my life and in the world, may you find me faithful in prayer and as a prayer.

356

Effective Prayer

*The prayer offered in faith will make the sick person
well; the Lord will raise them up. If they have sinned,
they will be forgiven. Therefore confess your sins to each
other and pray for each other so that you may be healed.
The prayer of a righteous person is powerful and effective.*

JAMES 5:15-16

Lord, I come to you today with my burden of sins. I hold each transgression up for a second look at my humanity. I place them in your light for a closer look at your grace. The practice of asking for forgiveness is important to my relationship with you. First, I am humbled and emptied of self. Then I am cleansed and filled with your mercy.

When I pray, Lord, I know you hear me. I become vulnerable in your presence because I have great faith in your protection. May you call me righteous, and may my prayers be deemed powerful and effective.

357

Where's My Worth?

*How can you believe if you accept praise
from one another but do not seek the glory
that comes from the only God?*

JOHN 5:44

My sense of self-worth rises too seldom and falls too easily. Constructive criticism from a friend or even a stranger can cause me to question my abilities. I can easily pick out what I don't like about my body or my looks. This is not how or who I want to be, Lord. And it is a disservice to all the blessings and strengths in my life.

Grant me a shift in perspective. When my thoughts are skewed and my sense of value is distorted by the world's view of perfection, show me how to receive the most important love of all—yours. Give me eyes to see my worth through your eyes and call it good, perfect, and whole.

358

In the Light

He gives wisdom to the wise
and knowledge to the discerning.
He reveals deep and hidden things;
he knows what lies in darkness,
and light dwells with him.

DANIEL 2:21-22

When there is darkness, you shed light. Where there is uncertainty, you remove the shadows. Where there is brokenness, you offer healing. Where deception is buried, you resurrect truth.

God, in every situation the brightness of your wisdom brings goodness and righteousness to light. Your Word is my source of knowledge and direction. Your never-changing precepts shape my perception of all that I experience.

359

A Process

You were taught, with regard to your former way of
life, to put off your old self, which is being corrupted
by its deceitful desires; to be made new in the attitude
of your minds; and to put on the new self, created
to be like God in true righteousness and holiness.

Ephesians 4:22-24

There is a process in place for change. God, you give me a path to newness in mind and spirit. You not only offer refreshment, but transformation as well. I can try something new—a hobby, a sport, a job—and even if the change is successful, it is temporary. But, Lord, your changes start from within and manifest in my life in different ways. They are there to stay, and they are intended to be with me forever.

I like how my mind works. There is great pleasure in learning, knowing, and growing in understanding. You allow for this deepening of my awareness and, in return, my life is changed and my thoughts shift from temporal to eternal.

360

Making a Way

*I am making a way in the wilderness
and streams in the wasteland.*

ISAIAH 43:19

I t is all I want, Lord—to make my way through this life with a sense of purpose and a perspective that reflects your heart for others. Because I am responsible for my earthly needs, I turn to you as my provider and my strength. There was a time when this caused me to be self-focused. I was forgetting that my life was intended for so much more.

My heart's desire is not to make *my* way through life, but to find *your* way to everlasting life. Carve out a path for the streams of the living water in the desert of my need. Deliver me from my selfishness so that I might discover the new things you have for me.

Serving Grace

*Each of you should use whatever gift you have
received to serve others, as faithful stewards
of God's grace in its various forms.*

1 PETER 4:10

Stepping out to serve you is not easy when I am called to do it on my own. I prefer the buddy system, and often you provide just the right person to join me for certain tasks or commitments. But there are also tugs at my heart that are for me alone. I sense you're leading me toward a particular way of serving you, but I'm scared to go it alone. Yet, my family and friends aren't called in this same direction, so it is time for me to step up and honor how you compel me forward.

Allow me to let go of my worries and lack of confidence so that I can adopt your strength and purpose. Maybe my presence will help others become involved. Maybe I will discover something about myself by following through with this impulse. No matter what, I know I will learn what faithfulness looks like.

362

Rich with Redemption

*In him we have redemption through his blood,
the forgiveness of sins, in accordance with the
riches of God's grace that he lavished on us.*

EPHESIANS 1:7-8

Keep me from being spiritually poor, Lord. In the material realm, I want for nothing. I have food to eat and a roof over my head. I have the means to care for my family. I even have tasted the luxury of abundance. But it takes wisdom to amass spiritual riches. Lead me to understand the treasures of salvation.

Your love inspires and satisfies me, Lord. I have been redeemed through the sacrifice of Christ. Your grace leads to spiritual riches. It multiplies to cover every one of my iniquities. My soul was purchased for a price, and it has made me a wealthy child of God.

363

I Work So Hard

It is by grace you have been saved, through faith—and this not from yourselves, it is the gift of God—not by works, so that no one can boast. For we are God's handiwork, created in Christ Jesus to do good works, which God prepared in advance for us to do.

EPHESIANS 2:8-10

I work so industriously, God. There is sweat on my brow as I survey the fruits of my labor. Signs of my hard work are everywhere. I dedicate the work of my hands to you. And yet, I resist the one thing you call me to do right now—fall to my knees and accept your grace. Why is that so difficult for me, Lord?

Soften my heart to receive your saving grace. Eliminate in me the need to earn your love. You freely give your grace so I can focus on doing the good works you have prepared for me. Grant me a deeper understanding of your provision. And receive my humble spirit as I rest in your mercy.

364

Approaching the Throne

*Let us then approach God's throne of grace with
confidence, so that we may receive mercy and
find grace to help us in our time of need.*

HEBREWS 4:16

I am stepping out in faith, Lord. I hold my hands out to you with expectation. Pour your grace over me. Let it cover me, fill me, and then overflow from me. I need you today, Lord, more than ever before. I walked around for months in false confidence based on my ability. It fell apart. As soon as one stone was cast at my facade, I came crumbling down in fragments of dust and pride.

Breathe your mercy into my soul. Let my body depend on it more than oxygen. Rebuild my life according to your plan. Only then can I return to you with confidence to ask for help, ask for your grace, ask to be whole.

365

First Things and Last Things

LORD, save us!
LORD, grant us success!
PSALM 118:25

God, is my desire for success pleasing to you? Am I keeping in line with your will? I start each day with good intentions, but I know that my own desires begin to dictate my decisions and the path of my success. I know that all good things are born of your heart. I know that my ability comes from you. Help me to always allow first things to remain first. Plant your priorities on my heart. Give me insight to see how to turn, how to lead, how to be. Grant me success as it pleases you, and not as it suits my five-year plan, Lord. I pray for your help because I no longer want to act as though this journey is one I make alone.

You, Lord, shape the first things and the last things. And all the wonders and joys in between. I'm so thankful that I can keep my eyes on you and align my steps with yours and not miss a thing.